Routledge Revivals

The Little Less

After the First World War, and partly because of it, nineteenth century capitalism began to be denounced by the critics both of the Left and of the Right- as an unintelligent system for producing too much of everything and for providing for the labour and capital engaged in the process a poor and unsatisfying level of rewards. Some adjustment was clearly called for. By tacit agreement between Left and Right, the various ingenious devices of economic restrictionism were introduced so as to induce people to produce a little less. By 1939, however, the spread of what may be called twentieth century collectivist capitalism began to disturb critiques of the Centre, who could not understand why everybody should expect to get a little more for producing a little less.

First published in 1947, *The Little Less* is intended to clarify the confusion of these claims and counter claims and to propose new economic goals for the post war period which avoid the economic frying pan as well as the fire. This is an important historical reference work for scholars and students of political economy.

The Little Less

An Essay in the Political Economy of Restrictionism

A. S. J. Baster

Routledge
Taylor & Francis Group

First published in 1947
by Methuen & Co Ltd.

This edition first published in 2025 by Routledge
4 Park Square, Milton Park, Abingdon, Oxon, OX14 4RN

and by Routledge
605 Third Avenue, New York, NY 10158

Routledge is an imprint of the Taylor & Francis Group, an informa business

Publisher's Note
The publisher has gone to great lengths to ensure the quality of this reprint but points out that some imperfections in the original copies may be apparent.

Disclaimer
The publisher has made every effort to trace copyright holders and welcomes correspondence from those they have been unable to contact.

A Library of Congress record exists under LCCN: 47024252

ISBN: 978-1-041-07757-2 (hbk)
ISBN: 978-1-003-64207-7 (ebk)
ISBN: 978-1-041-07758-9 (pbk)

Book DOI 10.4324/9781003642077

THE LITTLE LESS

An Essay in the Political Economy of Restrictionism

BY

A. S. J. BASTER

'Oh, the little more and how much it is
And the little less and what worlds away.'

METHUEN & CO. LTD. LONDON
36 Essex Street, Strand, W.C.2

First published in 1947

CATALOGUE NO. 3991/U

THIS BOOK IS PRODUCED IN COMPLETE CONFORMITY WITH THE AUTHORISED ECONOMY STANDARDS

PREFACE

THE tradition that as a subject of study political economy is dull and dreary may be said to have been originated about the time of Dickens, continued with success by the currency pamphleteers, and nobly maintained in our own time by the authors of Government Blue Books and some of the most eminent scholars in many countries. With the exception of certain gruesome modern works in semi-mathematical form, which have an austere charm of their own, it is generally thought of the ordinary run of writings on this subject that the aridity and obscurity of the text are in direct proportion to the importance of the subject-matter.[1]

The present book is a deliberate attempt to say something of importance on the subject in a way which makes it accessible to the general reader ignorant of the technical jargon. Its claim on public attention is, however, very modest, and its form is deliberately that of an essay in under-statement. Its essential lesson is not that a knowledge of political economy will make men better, but that ignorance of it may cost them dear. Up to the present, the chief non-specialist interest in the economic problems of the

[1] Pre-war writings on Savings and Investment reached a high level in both respects, though eventually even the principal contestants began to show signs of weakening and general bewilderment. Thus: 'Mr. Keynes finds fault with my statement that he has defined saving and investment as " two different names for the same thing ". . . . He himself describes them as being " for the community as a whole merely different aspects of the same thing ". If, as I suppose, we both mean the same thing by the same thing the distinction is rather a fine one' (Hawtrey, 'Alternative Theories of the Rate of Interest', *Economic Journal*, September 1937).

post-war period has come from those with axes to grind. Of the few great souls who, without pecuniary interest or special training, have struggled through the formidable and sometimes terrifying works of the classical authorities, some have unfortunately developed mental aberrations of the type common amongst second-year undergraduates in the subject, but more have fallen by the wayside defeated. If economic problems are as important as this book suggests, this is a dangerous state of affairs. The cure lies obviously in still more careful and painstaking attempts to build up an informed and watchful public opinion, with due regard to the fact that eternal vigilance is a tiresome and exhausting state of mind and that the Common Man has many pressing cares. This is such an attempt.

The book could perhaps have been longer with advantage. It is compressed not only for obvious reasons of the difficulties connected with production and reading at the present time, but also because it attempts to discover in the general reader's mind what is probably already there, buried under Heaven knows what heaps of economic quackery, and everywhere overlaid with the snap judgements of the daily press. The argument of the book, which is the result of several years reflection, owes much to controversies and observations at Geneva before the war, when the author was Economist at the International Labour Office. Geneva, whatever its shortcomings as a world peace centre before 1939, was an admirable listening-post. A hint of astringency here and there in the text may partly be explained by a highly educative period which the author spent in Whitehall as Economist to the Minister without Portfolio, who was in charge of reconstruction studies in 1941–3.

CONTENTS

CHAP. PAGE

PREFACE v

I. INTRODUCTORY

1. ECONOMIC DEMOBILIZATION AFTER 1918 1

II. THE LUNATIC YEARS

2. PRODUCING LESS 17
3. GROWING LESS 36
4. WORKING LESS 50
5. TRANSPORTING LESS 61
6. TRADING LESS 67
7. THE POLITICS OF RESTRICTIONISM 85

III. THE YEARS TO COME

8. THE POLITICAL ECONOMY OF FREEDOM 111
9. PRESENT PROSPECTS 151

I. INTRODUCTORY

CHAPTER I

ECONOMIC DEMOBILIZATION AFTER 1918

FOR the second time in this generation the world sets hope against experience and seeks escape from the anxieties of the present and the disasters of the recent past in the promise of peace and reconstruction after the war. In the Press the mood of the plain man everywhere is represented as one of great expectation sharpened by long-endured privations; but there is no need to dig very far beneath the comfortable level of simplification of the current Press campaigns to find bitter memories of the general disillusion in the years after the first World War and the general bewilderment in the years before the second. It is a question whether hope may be lightly cast down for the second time in twenty-five years and the Great Peace survive.

It is perhaps the most singular testimony to the basic optimism of the human race that the conviction could, in view of recent experience, ever become so widespread that a new world can be built after an outburst, lasting several years, of the most shocking savagery and the most appalling destruction on the greatest scale ever known. Unwarranted optimism in this matter is no doubt a necessary condition, though not, as some appear to believe, a sufficient condition for the survival of the race; but it ought not to be allowed to cloud judgement. The likelihood is, unfortunately, only too plain that in the years after the war, problems of the most baffling complexity will call for solution in an atmosphere as unfavourable as it could well be to reasonable discussion amongst men of goodwill. In British politics, restraints on the party struggle, imperfectly enforced in war-time, are not likely to be taken more seriously when the life of the nation is no longer threatened and parliamentary gladiators can once more abandon themselves to the heady delights of criticism without responsibility, on the pre-war model.

And it may be predicted with some confidence that in the hot-house atmosphere of victory, when everything seems possible and the inspired legislator prepares to right all the ancient wrongs of mankind by a few strokes of the pen, all sorts of odd-looking plants will bloom and flourish for his ensnarement. Only by their fruits in the chilly season to follow will they be known.

To judge from present tendencies, the primary mistake of judgement will be to underrate the lessons of the recent past. The experiences of the years after the last world war have not yet reached the comfortable stage of definitive interpretation in the school history books; they are in the memory of the living generation with a lively sense of its misfortunes at that time. And, as so often happens, the distortions of view at short distances have produced a tendency not only to disparage the inferior statesmanship of the past, but also to assume that the highest present wisdom is to-day the opposite of what was done before. The bearing of what was done before, and within living memory, on what will soon be attempted is in any case so evidently close that no apology is needed for a preliminary sketch of the economic problems of the years immediately following the Armistice of November 1918, and of the measures adopted for dealing with them.

The weary titans now perched high in the seats of power of the United Nations may be excused their moments of misgivings when they contemplate the task of unwinding the complex web of the war economy fabricated with such infinite labour under their direction. But to their predecessors in 1918, whose precedents were not twenty-five but a hundred years old, the problems must have seemed simply terrifying. The mere task of demobilizing an army of millions as a disciplined force—the concentration, sorting, feeding, housing and transport of millions of men moving from battle areas, from training grounds, and from prison camps to distant parts of the world, the reversal of the vast flow of armaments and equipment to the various fronts and the dispersal or destruction of immense stores on the spot—all this must surely have inspired an occasional nightmare even in the exultant autumn of 1918. Some may have known Slater's grim story[1] of demobilization after the Napoleonic Wars, when veterans from the Scottish Highlands were landed at Southampton and left to tramp slowly northwards. Starving, tattered and footsore, they reached the little crofts they had left years before only to find their old habitations vanished and their relations and neighbours driven away by wholesale evictions carried out by 'improving' landlords. It was clear that *this* sort of story could not be repeated in 1918.

The central fact of the post-Armistice period is that for a whole year after the Armistice millions of people were poured out of the armies and the munitions factories in this country at a rate which soon reached many thousands per day, and that during that year the recorded figures of unemployment never remotely compared with those common in the subsequent trade depressions of so-called normal times. In 1918 it was anticipated that apart from the problem of transferring over four million men from the Armed Services into peace-time work, over a million civilian war workers in the munitions industries would lose their jobs as a result of the cessation of war orders. In

[1] Slater, 'Poverty and the State', London, 1930, p. 400.

addition, half-a-million dilutees, mainly women, were due for discharge when the men returned and pre-war trade union practices were resumed.[1] Gradual discharge of the Armed Forces in accordance with industrial need [2] proved impossible to enforce in practice—the men began to walk out in defiance of orders. Gradual discharge of munition workers was not even attempted, for obvious reasons. Experienced contemporary observers may thus be excused for thinking, as they did then, that the menacing shadow of mass unemployment would fall on the Peace Conference at a crucial stage in its deliberations. Present-day authorities cannot be excused for ignoring the all-important fact that it did not. At no time during the year after the Armistice did the numbers of ex-Servicemen and civilian beneficiaries of out-of-work donation exceed 1,100,000, and by October 1919 just before the civilian benefit ceased the number was below 500,000. During all this time men were leaving the Armed Forces in tens of thousands *per day*, and in January 1919 the average daily rate of demobilization rose to a peak of 30,000. It is a striking fact that in twelve months the economic system absorbed nearly twice as many people as were unemployed on the average during the bad years of the Great Depression 1931–32, and that at its worst, unemployment during the immediate post-war period was hardly above one-third of what it subsequently became in the worst months of 1932.

The plain man is, at first sight, tempted to explain these striking facts by reference to the very considerable technical

[1] 'Official History of the British Ministry of Munitions', vol. vi, Part 2. Cf. Reports of the Civil War Workers Committee, Ministry of Reconstruction, 1918.

[2] i.e., men for the demobilization service first, 'pivotal' workers for various large industries next, and 'slip' men, demanded by employers whose peace-time production was held up for lack of labour, afterwards. *Vide* 'Reports of the Ministry of Reconstruction', Cd. 9231, 1918.

ingenuity displayed at the time in turning the machinery and manufacturing capacity of the armaments and allied industries over to peace-time production. The story of how motor-cars were turned out instead of howitzers, cash registers instead of gun-sights, beer engines instead of aeroplane motors, dyestuffs, rayon and fertilizers instead of explosives and poison gas,[1] makes the classical process of beating swords into ploughshares sound archaic and amateurish indeed. Did not Woolwich Arsenal itself turn over to the manufacture of railway wagons and milk-churns for a short time after the Armistice? Even Krupps ingeniously and reassuringly advertised all the most harmless and necessary kinds of steel goods, from railway engines to non-rusting artificial teeth (' guaranteed tasteless ').[2] Nevertheless, the belief that economic demobilization is an engineering job is a little naïve.

The ingenuity of the engineers, however admirable and necessary, was, as always, only the servant of economic necessity. The goods had to be sold; employers and workers had to earn their keep; and prices had to be sufficient to cover costs. After four years of war it was not at first obvious who was going to buy what goods and in what quantities. More precisely, the only guide available to the probable structure of the British industrial system in 1919 was the not very relevant record of what it was like before an economic earthquake occurred five years previously. On this question the engineers were out of court, the business men unreliable, and the Government conscious only of the most diverse alternative possibilities.

There were some half-hearted discussions of plans for a Ministry of Supply to fill Government requirements of various commodities in peace-time. A few orders were

1 ' Official History of the British Ministry of Munitions ', vol. VI.

2 ' Die Stellung der Grostadt Essen ', Statistisches Amt, Essen, 1929; ' Krupp ', Bernard Menne, p. 50.

given for steel and copper in semi-fabricated form likely to be required in the reconstruction period, and there was the elaborate demobilization plan, based on the order in which it was thought workers would be required. But at the back of these measures there lay no systematic view of the appropriate distribution of the national resources between particular industries, and the plan, which might have required such a view, ultimately broke down in face of the single-minded determination of the armies to get home as quickly as possible, official plans and exhortations notwithstanding. At a comparatively early date the opinion seems to have gained ground that people would demobilize and resettle themselves if a reasonable amount of freedom was allowed them to do so, and that the proper role of Government was to make provision for those who would not fit in.

No doubt the acceptance of this view owed much to the pressure of business men, who were anxious to regain economic powers they had lost during the war, and who feared a continuation of restrictions if demobilization and resettlement had proceeded according to a Government plan. It may also be that the stoutest authoritarian heart quailed before the sheer administrative difficulty at that time of directing five or six million people to work in particular jobs and 100,000 firms to produce particular commodities. In the event the authorities moved quickly, though not, it may be fairly assumed, without secret and gloomy forebodings. In order to minimize the waste of raw material, the Government terminated over three-quarters of all munitions contracts in the first two months after the Armistice, and the millions streaming out of the armies were joined by the millions from the armament factories. Controls over labour were relinquished at an early stage, though it would be disingenuous to pretend that in the public temper of 1918 the Government had much choice in this matter. With unequivocal support from the business community the Government then quickly relaxed the various controls over foreign trade, raw material allocation, building, the use of factory space, dealing in essential commodities, and all the rest of the economic apparatus of war-time, which by the autumn of 1919 had, for the most part, disappeared.[1]

It would be wrong to give an impression in this matter of a deliberate long-considered act of policy which had already run the gauntlet of public debate. Just as the country as a whole was never convinced of the necessity for systematic economic controls for the organization of the war economy itself, so equally there was no great debate of control versus the free economy which got beyond the level of unanswered assertions by business men that Government controls got in their way. The Defence of the Realm Act, under which most of the controls were set up, provided that Orders in Council under it could be issued only during the war. As the war with Germany ended officially on 10 January, 1920, the path of least resistance was to do nothing, so that most of the controls which had not been abolished already, disappeared then. It was similarly much easier to shut down the new Ministries of Food, of Shipping and of Munitions than to carry them on, as they likewise had been set up by their constituent Acts for the period of the war.

Many important controls—e.g., those over the use of iron and steel, non-ferrous metals, and industrial chemicals—were suspended before the end of 1918, though iron and steel subsidies were continued for a short time afterwards. Priority certificates for manufactured goods ceased to be necessary after 1919. Most of the 250 national factories were disposed of privately after schemes for their operation

[1] Tawney, 'The Abolition of Economic Controls, 1918–21', *Economic History Review*, 1943.

by Government to relieve unemployment had been rejected. At the same time as controls over the handling of goods were dropped controls over prices were relaxed too, though some subsidies, particularly food subsidies, continued, and housing subsidies became a new feature of the post-war period. Derationing of food came about in stages after a false start due to unforeseen shortages of sugar and meat, and most foods could be purchased free of rationing by the middle of 1920.

Having cleared the economic decks for action, the Government made a certain provision for casualties by starting a special Out-of-Work Donation Scheme for those who did not succeed in finding jobs, and by legislating for the temporary maintenance of war-time wage rates for those who did. In addition, there were various educational and training schemes for ex-soldiers and civilian war workers. But, beyond this, people were expected to re-settle themselves, prices, employment, and production to find their own level, and capital to flow into industries which business men thought likely to be most profitable.

At first this policy produced a boom which carried the employment burden of the demobilization period with comparative ease. Business men discovered that, to begin with, there was an insatiable public demand for almost everything. Industrialists wanted new buildings put up and worn-out machinery replaced. Railway companies wanted quantities of new rolling-stock and years of deferred maintenance made good, and traders wanted to rebuild their stocks. Private consumers wanted new houses, motor-cars, clothes, and all the things they had been deprived of during the war. The significant fact is that in most cases the pressure of accumulated demand was matched by accumulated money savings built up deliberately against the time of rehabilitation, or accumulated willy-nilly by the normally improvident for want of a spending outlet during war-time. Thus, in the comparatively free market conditions established in the second half of 1919, the business of renewing and patching up the nation's productive equipment flourished for practically the entire period during which substantial demobilization was proceeding—in spite of the congested transport system, exhausted labour, a serious dearth of skilled men, coal-mining strikes, raw materials scarcities, and the delays involved in re-assembling machinery for new processes.

The lifting of the controls meant, no doubt, that the post-war plans for reconstruction activity got under way more quickly; but it is impossible to deny that the turnover was greatly facilitated by a rapidly rising wholesale price level beginning in the spring of 1919 and in its later stages, particularly at the end of 1919, becoming definitely inflationary—i.e., involving increases in the money supply *not* associated with increases in employment. Nothing is easier for the pundits at this distance than to show that the Government should have intervened at an earlier stage than it did to prevent undue inflation of the price level by the operation of the controls which remained to it, particularly control over the short-term rate of interest. But the uncomfortable legacy of war finance, in the shape of a floating debt of £1200 millions, and the absence of the stringent controls of war-time over physical goods, made the task of successful intervention a formidable one. Moreover, it would have taken considerable political courage to interfere with the rapid revival of business then going on and take the risk of slowing down the absorption of the unemployed. In the event, prices got out of hand and there was a rise in the wholesale level of approximately 30 per cent above the Armistice level from July 1919 to April 1920, supported by a more than proportionate increase in bank advances. Rising prices stimulated further buying, until the familiar spiral was generated. Wages rose and wage disbursements increased, and speculative capital flotations, especially in Lancashire textiles, were multiplied on the basis of extravagant profit expectations.

Discussions of why the boom broke, though of a certain melancholy academic interest, are unprofitable from the present point of view. The fact was that when it did break, and the economic indices started their spiral downward plunge, the activity resulting from the demand for renewals and re-stocking had exhausted itself, and the real trials of reconstruction for the British economic system, which had been merely postponed for a short breathing space, had now to be faced against the unpromising background of a deflationist crisis of world-wide dimensions. A number of problems which would have been awkward in any case were now elevated to the status of a Gordian knot, and, as will be shown in the sequel, received the appropriate treatment. Whether the authorities could have intervened at the right moment with a nice mixture of encouragement for normal business together with restraint on inflation is not certain. What is clear is that the real business of economic reconstruction was made insuperably difficult by the runaway monetary factor in 1919–20.[1]

A striking illustration of this is provided by the post-war development of the building industry. Although house-building during the war had practically ceased, and the shortage in 1919 was estimated at nearly half a million houses, there was no post-war boom in the building industry, which in fact produced considerably less than its pre-war output until the Government subsidy schemes were put into operation. The shortage of skilled labour no doubt explains this in part. 'Only in 1924 did the building unions relax their admission requirements in return for

[1] Cf. Pigou, 'The Transition from War to Peace', Oxford, 1943, pp. 13–18.

an undertaking on the part of the Government to continue building subsidies for fifteen years.'[1] But the chief reason was that house-building ceased to be a profitable occupation in the post-war period because the Government fixed maximum rents with the laudable object of insulating housing accommodation from the effects of inflation. The maxima were, unfortunately—and perhaps unavoidably—fixed too low.

Even apart from the monetary complication, the post-war conversion problem for several major industries was a formidable one. Steel-makers, for example, in 1919 had to find outlets for a total ingot capacity of twelve million tons—half as much again as in 1913. Rolling-mill capacity was equally redundant. The submarine losses of 1917 had led to such intense efforts to increase shipbuilding that steel-milling capacity for ship plates, as well as for shell steel, &c., had increased by 50 per cent at the end of the war,[2] by which time, however, the shipbuilding industry itself was on the verge of a catastrophic slump. As might have been expected, the shipbuilding situation was quite abnormal.[3] While the size of the world's mercantile marine was not greatly different at the end of the war from what it had been in 1914, shipbuilding capacity was twice as large, and continued to increase after 1919 in view of high and rising freights. The rise was temporary, and due in large part to port congestion, and the inevitable slump in the freight market which began in the spring of 1920

[1] 'Economic Fluctuations in the U.S. and the U.K. 1918–22', League of Nations, Geneva, 1942, p. 68.

[2] Clay, 'The Post-War Unemployment Problem', London, 1929, p. 85; Layton, 'The Influence of the War on the British Iron and Steel Industry', *Manchester Guardian Reconstruction Supplement*, 7 Sept. 1922, p. 438.

[3] Salter, 'Allied Shipping Control', Oxford, 1921, p. 218; Robertson, 'The Slump in Shipping', *Manchester Guardian Reconstruction Supplement*, 18 May 1922, p. 71.

brought annual construction in British yards from 708,000 tons down to 55,000 tons in two years.

In view of the marked dependence of the staple British industries, particularly coal, cotton, and engineering, on export markets, readjustment of the industrial structure to the changed economic conditions overseas would have been difficult enough even under the wisest monetary management. In no country, least of all in Great Britain, did the task of adaptation go on in a vacuum. It went on in an economic world where old-established channels of trade were cut across in many directions by the territorial provisions of the Peace Treaties, where political stability was in many countries precarious, where international economic relationships were profoundly influenced by reparations and inter-Allied debt payments, and where Government finances were, with few exceptions, completely disorganized by the financial legacy of the war. It was in this unpromising situation that the British Government decided to re-establish the gold standard at the pre-war parity. Official acceptance of the Cunliffe Committee's recommendations in 1919 in favour of gradual deflation of the price level showed that the Government meant business in this matter. Unfortunately the evidence is [1] that, in anticipation of the return to gold, the foreign exchange value of sterling was forced up too far and too fast by speculators discounting a rise. Exporters were thus faced with the severe handicap of an 'over-valued' pound, in addition to their other difficulties. The resultant changes in the pattern of British exports after 1918 are not surprising.

In 1919 more than a half of all British exports went to Europe, as against one-third in 1913. British trade with long-established markets in India, the Far East, and Latin America, however, lost its pre-war importance. American trade with the Far East and with Europe increased, but

[1] Cf. Gregory, 'The Return to Gold', London, 1925.

trade with the British Empire fell off. Measured in quantities, total British exports at the lowest post-war level in 1921 were a half of what they had been in 1913.

The staple exports felt these changes keenly. Coal exports were maintained for a time, mainly as a result of the French invasion of the Ruhr in 1923. But the competition of alternative fuels, perceptible before the war, made itself strongly felt soon afterwards. The textile trades, which were regarded as of such special importance after the Armistice, as an alternative employment for women discharged from filling factories, that high priorities were given to raw cotton imports, proved in the event a broken reed. Before the war, textiles were the most important United Kingdom export, and only about one quarter of the total production was consumed at home. In 1921 exports of cotton piece-goods had fallen to less than half the pre-war quantity. Buyers in an impoverished and nationalistic world either made shift with the local product in their own countries, which had been artificially stimulated in many cases during the war, or turned to the cheaper varieties from Japan.

From the British point of view, the misfortunes of the post-war period must be ascribed to a tragic mixture of the consequences of wrong decisions, particularly in the monetary field, with the appalling and quite inevitable difficulties of industrial conversion in a strange, new, and distinctly uncongenial economic world. The chief mistake was not the removal of controls itself, for which it is now so fashionable to chide our fathers; it was rather the mistake of trying to unwind the tightly controlled economic system of 1918 in a few months of hasty legislation, with the hope that in the mere absence of restraint from the Government, private interest would do whatever was necessary to restore normal—that is, pre-1914—conditions.

The danger of this course was much increased when the

large-scale unemployment of the post-war period, which had long haunted the thoughts of those responsible for reconstruction plans, failed at first sight to appear. It may be guessed that it was perhaps at this point that there originated amongst those in authority the insidious habit of taking a hasty glance at the unemployment figures and assuming that at anything under a million God's in His Heaven and all's right with the economic world. Any such hasty glances in 1919 would, of course, have been highly encouraging. But few would now deny that the unemployment index at that time gave a completely misleading picture of the trend of the underlying economic forces.

At any rate, there was no serious attempt to deal immediately after the war with the drastic changes in what may be called the chief British economic landmarks, both at home and abroad, and, in particular, there was no attempt at that time to face up to the problem of the excess productive capacity created for war-time purposes. These problems were left to be solved piecemeal, under the most unfavourable conditions, during the period between the two wars.

These considerations explain, though they do not excuse, the peculiar aberrations of economic policy during this period. The policy-makers did not start with a clean sheet. They were constantly grappling with the vestigials of the problem of economic demobilization after 1918. And there was a further inheritance from war-time which ultimately came to have a very significant influence on post-war policy. Government officials and business men—the natural enemies of the nineteenth-century economic scene—got the unusual experience of working in harness together and of discovering that at many points their interests converged. There is no doubt that this experience left a deep impression in the minds of both parties.

As the post-war years receded the general conclusion gradually formed in the public mind that the liberal economic system had failed. It was certainly true that the economic system of 1919, unaided by controls, had failed to accommodate itself to changes, similar in magnitude but opposite in direction to those of 1914, which had forced the suspension of economic freedom almost *in toto*. Most people, however, were satisfied with the more understandable view, which certainly had the merit of acceptability in terms of prevailing political dogma. Living through the years of disillusionment following the short-lived post-war boom, they felt themselves repeatedly baulked by the long-continued and puzzling intractability of the economic problems of the time, and they began to ask whether the 'free' economic system to which there had been such a hasty return after 1918, ought not to be abandoned altogether. Those in search of a new economic philosophy found many practical pointers in the operation of the war economy by Government and business men in the years 1914–18. A new and ingenious, if sometimes quaint and surprising philosophy did, indeed, come to fascinate and dominate public opinion in the decade before the Second World War, and bids fair to become the touchstone of Government policy in the decade after it. It is the true inwardness of this new gospel and its implications in the sphere of practical politics which it is now proposed to examine.

II. THE LUNATIC YEARS

CHAPTER 2

PRODUCING LESS

THERE is some warrant for the view that the whole corpus of economic theory, from the Law of Diminishing Utility onwards, could be deduced from a diligent study of the implications of the depressing but reliable maxim that one can have too much of a good thing.[1] Few business men, it may safely be said, have followed this difficult and somewhat stony path very far; but most appear to have arrived at the point of a firm grasp of the important converse principle that the less people have of anything, the more, in general, they are willing to pay for it.

It must be conceded that many arrive at this point without much deep reflection. Long and disappointing experience has shown them that the more they produce, the more the price goes down. Other things being equal, increased production is therefore bad for them, and bad for everyone else in the trade. Doubtless it was some such line of thought as this which led to the view, so widespread before the war, that the chief economic problem (on which orthodox economists were exasperatingly vague) was how to increase employment without increasing production.

Natural though this sort of argument may sound in the mouths of producers, it has generally seemed desirable for some safeguard to be set up in the public interest to prevent them from following it to its logical conclusion. This

[1] Cf. L. V. Birck, 'Theory of Marginal Value', London, 1922, c. 1. Professor Birck proves that Faust's exclamation 'Oh! stay, stay for ever, happy hour!', could not have been seriously intended.

would involve restricting output to the point which maximizes producers' profits, leaves the consumer with fewer and worse goods, and encumbers the economic system with productive capacity (including labour) which is not fully used. The normal safeguard is the provision for systematic competition amongst producers so as to induce them to exert themselves in rivalry with one another to furnish the needs of the public in the most efficient way. Naturally, any such competition for public favour, like any other contest where the aim is not merely fighting for its own sake, has to be conducted according to rules; and in this case it seems obvious to common sense that the object of the rules ought to be to discover who is best fitted to serve the public with what. In practice, however, and for reasons to be discussed, the resemblance between this sort of conception and what was called the competitive system before the war was hidden from any but rather determined and advanced students of the subject, and even denied altogether by some of them.

The principles of the pre-war system certainly seem at first sight to have originated from a re-discovery of the fact that production is economically ruinous to producers. Only on some such hypothesis as this is it possible to explain why Governments and organized producers applied themselves with such energy and ingenuity to discouraging and thwarting what obviously seemed to them the rather shady and disreputable business of increasing what used to be called the wealth of nations. Sometimes the discouragement was applied early enough to prevent any such activity taking place at all, as when in England people were paid weekly sums by the Government on the strict understanding that they did no work whatever.[1] Sometimes producers

[1] The condition sounds dubious to common sense and is not justified analytically. Cf. J. Robinson, 'Essays in the Theory of Employment', London, 1937, p. 101.

were paid to stop before their jobs were properly finished, as when in America pigs were 'rendered into grease and fertilizer tankage' instead of into pork.[1] But in very many cases Government was called in at the eleventh hour to deal with a catastrophe provoked by the bounty of Nature joined with the irresponsibility of Man and too far gone for any but the sternest measures. In Brazil, where some interesting experiments with such measures were made, heaps of coffee were soaked in petrol and set alight.[2]

The results of these efforts on the prices of the commodities affected revealed a further economic harmony which must have been most gratifying to the protagonists of this policy. They rose. Now, in 1933, certain Governments had already committed themselves to the view that 'a rise throughout the world in the general level of wholesale prices is in the highest degree desirable'.[3] Higher prices, as the British Chancellor of the Exchequer pointed out, would make business more profitable; and business would expand, and so relieve unemployment.[4] What clearer proof could there be of the wisdom of restricting production than that its result should be a rise of prices? The authorities were not slow to see this fortunate connexion. If these restrictionist experiments succeed, said the Chancellor of the Exchequer, 'we shall have had an object lesson well worth very serious consideration in trying to think how it is possible to raise the wholesale commodity prices of the world'. To uncharitable critics this singular line of argument appears to prove that the proper means of producing an expansion of industry is to contract it. The

1 'Report of the U.S. Agricultural Adjustment Administration', 1933–4, p. 117.

2 J. W. F. Rowe, 'Markets and Men', Cambridge, 1936, p. 22.

3 British Empire Currency Declaration at the World Economic Conference, 1933.

4 A. C. Pigou, 'Economics in Practice', London, 1935, p. 143.

less censorious may permit themselves the reflection that the argument was not altogether borne out by experience.

It is safe to say that the Chancellor and those with him who held that the competitive system should be replaced by a system of organized restrictions on production were converted to these views long before 1933. In fact it is a matter of some difficulty to state precisely when it was decided to give up the attempt to make the competitive system work. The law on the matter became tolerably clear as to principles at quite an early stage in the development of the British industrial system. From Stuart times onwards the grant of monopoly rights in particular trades by the Crown provides a fair example of restrictionism in operation. These grants led to such abuses that the common law rule became established that 'public policy demands from every man the free exercise of his trade in the public interest'[1] and various legal barriers were consequently set up against 'restraint of trade', meaning practices which restrained employers or workers from competing against each other. It is not without significance, particularly for the many who assume that their own age is exceptional, to record that these barriers lasted until almost the end of the nineteenth century.

Breaches were first made on behalf of combinations of workers in restraint of trade—that is to say, Trade Unions—which were exempted on the ground of the weak bargaining position of the workers. Restraints of trade which were 'reasonable' in relation to what the judges thought was the public interest were then freed from the ban. After the Mogul Steamship Company's case in 1892[2] the legal view of the degree of monopoly which was required in the

[1] Cooke, 'Legal Rule and Restraint of Trade', *Economic Journal*, March 1936.

[2] Mogul Steamship Company *v.* McGregor, Gow & Co. A.C. 25 (1892).

public interest broadened considerably, on the basis of a statement by the judge that 'if peaceable and honest combinations of capital for purposes of trade competition are to be struck at, it must, I think, be by legislation, for I do not see that they are under the ban of the Common Law'. For all practical purposes the old view that monopoly is destructive of the public interest ceased to be held in this country by the end of the nineteenth century, and before the Second World War it was possible to say, in a broad survey of the situation,[1] that 'there is not a single modern case in which a trade protection agreement has been upset on grounds of public policy'. A straw indicating that the wind was in quite another direction was provided in 1939 by the dictum of the Manchester magistrate that 'if only the public would realize that in buying at these cut-price shops they are lending their help to criminal activities, they would think more carefully about where they buy'.[2] Admirers of the law of the Medes and Persians, which changeth not, may well feel some alarm at the prospect of the law which once protected the public against monopolies being used in the future to protect monopolies against the public. It is not easy to prove that their fears are exaggerated.

THE ORGANIZATION OF INDUSTRY BEFORE THE WAR

At the end of the last war the Committee on Trusts reported that 'we are satisfied that Trade Associations and combines are rapidly increasing in this country, and may within no distant period exercise a paramount control over all important branches of British trade'.[3] In one important respect the Committee would, no doubt, wish to amend

[1] Articles on 'Restraint of Trade' in *Manchester Guardian*, 27 August 1937.

[2] *Economist*, 6 May 1939.

[3] 'Report of the Committee on Trusts', Cd. 9236, 1919, p. 11.

their Report if they had been called together in 1939—they would have added to their list of monopolies, after some anxious reconsideration of their recommendations, the statutory monopolies in coal-mining and agriculture set up by Government and the encouragement given by Government to various forms of combination in textiles, iron and steel, and shipping. An unprejudiced observer from Mars might have been excused before the war if he had reported that, contrary to what he had read in the text-books, production was not organized competitively by business men working for private profit, but by Government Departments, Marketing Boards, Statutory Monopolies, Trusts, Cartels, and Trade Associations, all working in the public interest.

It is true that the organizing tended to be rather piecemeal, and that many of these bodies were but indifferently co-ordinated. For example, there are stories of the Whisky Trust falling out with the Glass Bottle ring, of shipbuilders disagreeing with shipowners, and of steelmakers failing to see completely eye to eye with motor-car manufacturers; and it is a safe assumption that not all of these stories can be apocryphal. A sympathetic observer from Mars might perhaps have attributed these shortcomings to the growing-pains of a new society. To such a one it might have appeared that by 1939, by and large, the 'planned economy' so long urged in principle and so ardently desired by such diverse sections of the population was within an ace of achievement. The less enthusiastic views of a somewhat nearer observer, from the United States, that the British were just 'planning to muddle',[1] or—most unkindest cut of all—that there was more 'plotting' than 'planning'

[1] 'England is experiencing nothing more "revolutionary" than a completely planless, muddling decline of competition . . . the British do not plan to plan; they plan to muddle!' 'Price and Production Control in British Industry', B. Lewis, Chicago, 1939, p. 32.

about it [1] would no doubt have been indignantly dismissed as lacking in sympathy and insight.

Certainly the charge of lack of insight would not have been difficult to substantiate against even the most acute observers, who, without the benefit of expert knowledge, had taken a first glance at the economic scene. It would not have been unnatural, for example, to begin by assuming that some idea of the structure of a particular industry could be got by setting down a list of the many hundreds of separate firms in it and assigning to each firm a place in the industry corresponding in importance to the size of its capital as shown in the annual balance sheet. Unfortunately, the modern invention of a device called the holding company has cast the shadow of dubiety on any such procedure. The ramifications of pre-war holding companies, which by the purchase of small blocks of voting shares in other companies secured a strategic control over entire industries, often defied understanding by their creators, their internal book-keeping and their real interrelations presenting complexities compared to which the genealogy of the patriarchs from Adam unto Noah is the essence of simplicity. In the absence of any economic equivalent of the prayer-book rules about marriage and consanguinity in the theological sphere, all sorts of monstrous financial unions were consummated, before which the pen falters and the understanding wilts. Sometimes, it is to be feared, the mantle of a famous name was used to cloak any financial unseemliness,[2] though it was not

[1] 'The English economy of to-day is a mixture of planning and plotting, with plotting predominating. . . . Fascism is . . . plotting which has been found out and has to justify itself. The institution of socialism may be said to depend upon successful plotting followed by successful planning.' 'Planning and Plotting', H. Smith, *Review of Economic Studies*, June 1936.

[2] Perhaps engaged through the medium of a small advertisement,

always clear that the bearer of it understood what was going on. Occasionally, as in the Unilever group [1] or in Imperial Chemicals,[2] the ramifications of these financial empires were more or less well known. But, generally, their precise boundaries, their internal strength, and financial stability were matters hidden from the curious.

It is noteworthy that as the result of the labours of two distinguished Committees (on one of which sat Lord Kylsant, Chairman of the Royal Mail Steam Packet Company) on the subject of the reform of company law, the Companies Act of 1928 was passed, providing for the admission of a little light into the economic darkness in which these giant concerns operated. One expert critic has referred to this procedure as a case of putting one or two odd locks on to the stable door, with great care not to frighten the various occupants after a substantial percentage of them had already got away beyond all hope of recovery.[3] In the proceedings which followed the collapse of the Royal Mail Steam Packet Company and its associated companies in 1932, there is admittedly a certain amount of material which justifies such a view.[4]

On one other aspect of the pre-war industrial system even the most diligent researchers might confess to certain doubts born of ignorance. These doubts arise in the matter of the exact difference between a Trade Association, formed, as the Statement of Objects so often indicates, 'to organize the Industry in the Public Service', and the old-

---

such as the following, which appeared in the *Daily Telegraph*, 4 October 1932:

'A TITLED GENTLEMAN is invited to communicate with a progressive company with a view to installing him as a director. Write A, Box 10, 161.'

[1] Cf. *Economist*, 11 June 1932.

[2] *Ibid.*, 19 January 1935.

[3] H. B. Samuel, 'Shareholders' Money', London, 1933, p. 3.

[4] *Idem*, op. cit., c. 12.

fashioned Trust, which used to be formed to exploit the public by creating artificial scarcities. Those who normally cannot distinguish a spade from a shovel are apt to point out that whereas the Trust used to find it difficult to make everybody in the trade join in, the Trade Association obtains the same result by getting the Government to pass a law making it illegal for anybody to stay out. This exaggeration cannot be dismissed as altogether pointless, but in practice it is more often the policy of a Trade Association to see what can be done by a little private pressure first, and to try to bring recruits in by making business impossible for them if they stay out. Thus the Association may try to control the distribution of the product at an early stage, so as to block the business of independents, by tying dealers with exclusive contracts, or by threatening boycotts, or by blacklisting.[1] If this procedure does not promise well, the Association, sometimes with Government support, may press a system of licensing on the trade, on the ostensible ground that trading standards need to be raised and protected against unscrupulous and untrained interlopers. Those who accepted this line of argument and the system it led to may have had some qualms at the wholehearted way it was adopted before the war, when licensing schemes were being pressed on a wide range of the most unlikely groups of traders, from the fried-fish and chip shops of Acton [2] to the clove dealers of Zanzibar.[3] And recent criticism can only be said to have added to their perplexities. The origin of the popularity of licensing, according to the critics, was not only, or not at all, that the trade desired to raise standards, but that

[1] H. Levy 'Retail Trade Associations', London, 1942, Part IV.

[2] All persons carrying on the business of fish-frying (white fish) were required to register with the White Fish Commission in 1938.

[3] In 1938 the Government of Zanzibar, supported by the Secretary of State, proposed a scheme to license clove dealers. *The Times*, 3 March 1938.

licensing is one of the infallible ways of restricting the number of entrants to the trade, of maintaining the profits of the old firms, and of insulating the trade from the play of outside competition.

It must be admitted that some colour is given to these perhaps unworthy suspicions by the practices of trading groups once they have become organized on an exclusionist basis. Their first business is to fix prices (or arrange a friendly interchange of information on prices between members) at what appears to them a reasonable level,[1] lay down uniform terms and conditions of sale, and levy heavy and apparently legitimate penalties on members who do not adhere to them, which puts the membership privilege on the same footing as the well-known device of giving the small boy a penny he doesn't really want so that it can be taken away from him when he is naughty.[2] It is sometimes a little difficult to distinguish these methods from those of a strongly entrenched monopoly. Thus the Electric Lamp Manufacturers' Association practically dictated the conditions of sale of electric lamps. The Proprietary Articles Trade Association, which includes about 400 manufacturers, 60 wholesalers, and 10,000 retailers in its membership, fixed wholesale and retail prices for about 10,000 articles sold in chemists' shops; and similar tactics were followed by the powerful Motor Traders' Association and the Cycle and Motor-Cycle Manufacturers' and Traders' Union for garage supplies.

[1] To show that 'reasonableness' is hardly an objective criterion for price-fixing, John Hilton in the Report of the Committee on Trusts (p. 24) quotes the story of the sour beer handed out free. Those who received it found it 'just right', i.e. 'if it had been any better we shouldn't ha' got it, and if it had been any worse, we couldn't ha' drunk it'.

[2] Illustrated in Thorne *v.* Motor Traders' Association (1937) A.C. 797. It was held that the demand of the Association for penalties from a recalcitrant member was not 'a demand for money with menaces without reasonable and proper cause'. The threat used was a commercial boycott.

However, in view of the extraordinary variety of Trade Associations and the widely differing scope of their functions on paper, if not of their objects in principle, the most useful approach is perhaps to discuss their activities in particular industries. Between the wars most branches of industry (and agriculture) were busy organizing representative bodies of one sort or another competent to speak or act on their behalf, and sometimes, empowered to make rules governing the conduct of business by member firms. In order to avoid being rushed into the conclusion that these bodies are, from their very nature, and despite the devotion they might profess to the public interest, bound inevitably to serve the sectional interests of their members in disregard of the public welfare where the two conflict, it is important to know something of their activities in specific cases.

What looks like a common pattern of behaviour is distinctly noticeable in certain industries—but it is not the old-fashioned pattern of producers' restrictionism which might have been expected by the simple-minded. This is not to say that the traditional expedients were disregarded. Minimum price-fixing, for example, was a very common function of these bodies, and was particularly widespread throughout manufacturing industry. The allocation of maximum output quotas was also a familiar line, strengthened, as in the tinplate industry, by a system of fines collected from firms rash enough to produce more than their quota, and paid over to those canny enough to go easy and produce less. Schemes for allocating maximum sales and geographical markets, as in brick-making, were also common. The new and far more effective principle, however, was to restrict output at its source—that is, to destroy the plant and machinery necessary to produce it.

Among the chief voluntary bodies formed on this basis there may be noted the Millers' Mutual Association, formed in 1929 to purchase and dismantle surplus milling capacity, and the Woolcombers Mutual Association, formed in

1933 to purchase and dismantle surplus woollen mills and resell the sites on condition that they were not further used for woolcombing. In 1930 a group including most of the shipbuilding firms in the country founded a company with the revealing title of National Shipbuilders Security, Ltd. The company was financed by a levy on new construction, and its function was to buy up and dismantle shipbuilding yards alleged to be obsolete or redundant. In four years the company had scrapped some 137 berths with a shipbuilding capacity of about one million tons. For the textile industry—an early but far from whole-hearted convert to these procedures—the Lancashire Cotton Corporation was formed in 1929 for the purpose *inter alia* of buying and breaking up redundant plant in the American spinning section.

The Government entered into the spirit of these arrangements with enthusiasm and some handsome contributions of cash from the public Treasury, which had the effect of stimulating the creation of representative trade bodies where none existed before. Thus, under the British Shipping (Assistance) Act of 1935, a Tramp Shipping Subsidy Committee was set up by the Government to distribute Government advances under the scrap-and-build scheme, which provided for the demolition of two gross tons of old shipping for every ton of new shipping built. In the first two years of the operation of the Act, the Committee distributed some £3½ millions in subsidies for the purpose of buying ships to scrap. A slight variation on this theme was provided in the tanker section, where the Government paid tanker owners a subsidy varying with the number of days on which their ships were *un*employed.[1] In Lancashire, the Government set up the Spindles Board in 1936 to purchase and scrap redundant spinning-plant, though the Board levied on the industry for its expenses.

By 1939 it must have seemed to the prophetically minded

[1] *Economica*, Feb. 1941, p. 68(n).

to be only a matter of time before all producers became convinced that there was too much of everything, and called on the Government for urgent action—either in the form of more taxes all round, so that everybody could be paid to produce less, or in the form of statutory monopolies for everything, so that everybody would pay higher prices in order that machinery might be destroyed and less produced. Converts in Lancashire, where old traditions died hard and opinion was at first sharply divided, became particularly numerous. The textile finishers' associations, notably the dyers and printers, produced independent schemes to regulate output, backed by provisions for the purchase and scrapping of redundant plant. 'Lancashire's Remedy', produced in 1936 at a meeting of the Joint Committee of Cotton Trade Organizations, proposed an Enabling Act under which schemes of reorganization supported by a majority in the trade could be applied compulsorily to all firms, the schemes to have as their major object the fixing of minimum prices and the destruction of surplus capacity.

In the light of these facts, it is a little difficult to avoid the conclusion that there is a certain family resemblance between the behaviour of these trade bodies and the policy which would have been pursued if the particular industries concerned had been dominated by one large firm—i.e. the fixing of prices so as to produce maximum monopoly profits, the consequential reduction of output, and the sterilization of productive capacity surplus to the smaller output. There is, of course, an important body of opinion, including owners of out-of-date machinery, who very naturally want to get the best price for it, and trade experts with their tongues in their cheeks, which holds that the destruction of old plant is a public service. If any machines are to be destroyed under redundancy schemes at all, it may be readily granted that the highest form of wisdom is to scrap the old ones first, and the new ones in due course afterwards. But the unkinder critics go to the length of denying the wisdom of destruction *in principle*. In their view any contribution to revenue which the use of an old machine brings over and above the prime costs of running it, justifies keeping it in use, both from the point of view of its owner or the consumer of its products; and, conversely, it is uneconomic to instal new machines until the total costs of operating them can be brought down below the prime costs of running the old ones. But these esoteric considerations, which are quite beyond all but those who have ever decided to go on using an old bicycle instead of buying a new one, are naturally of small moment if the Government can be persuaded to pay part of the cost of the new machines or allow prices to the consumer to be fixed high enough to cover whatever costs may have been incurred in installing them.

COAL

In the case of the coal industry, an impressive array of representative trade bodies was set up on lines recalling those in other industries; but an interesting attempt was made to meet the charge of monopoly in advance by preserving a sort of vestigial competition, not between single firms, but between blocks of firms grouped into cartels or district selling associations. As each district fixed its own price without regard to the others, the resultant competition sometimes had the embarrassing result that one district complained of 'unfair' competition from another. Although it is an exaggeration to claim that the scheme made it profitable to send coals to Newcastle, Scottish coal, for example, frequently undercut Midland coal in the Lancashire and Southern markets, no doubt to the substantial relief of unemployment on the railways. Moreover, by a curious coincidence, internal prices in some districts were fixed so high that the exporting areas, selling competitively in the world market, more than once showed a strong desire to seek outlets in the more congenial economic climate of the home market, or to press for a subsidy scheme for exports based on a levy spread over the whole industry.

It is true that the districts were not free to fix contracts entirely as they pleased. But the intervention of the co-ordinating body—namely, the Central Mining Council—was not always attended with the happiest results. Thus in 1936 the Anglo-Iranian Oil Company and the Low Temperature Carbonization Company offered very large seven- and twenty-five-year coal contracts to the South Wales Mining District, where the depression had been very severely felt. The District accepted, but was overruled by the Central Council on the ground that 'it is its duty to secure an economic price for coal' and 'this duty could not be carried out if there were to be freedom to make contracts of unlimited duration'.[1] In sum, those who got the impression that 'district competition' combined the worst of two worlds were perhaps not entirely wrong. It did not deceive those who wanted the real thing, whilst it merely irritated those who, for creditable reasons or otherwise, wanted a national plan for the whole industry (i.e., a national monopoly) with 'co-ordination of prices' to suit.

Within each district, where competition had been abolished, production quotas were distributed between firms; but owners having no further taste for what had become a somewhat troublesome business could sell their quotas to their more determined and successful colleagues (whose prices to the consumer rose correspondingly), close their pits, and retire in peace. Buyers often found this a convenient arrangement, as their own quotas sometimes showed drastic reductions on previous production. Thus in one case a colliery capable of producing 1,000 tons

[1] *Economist*, 26 December 1936, p. 632.

quarterly was fined at the rate of half-a-crown per ton for any excess production over 4 tons;[1] and the Askern Coal and Iron Company, capable of working profitably in 1932 at an output of 16,000 tons weekly, was allowed to produce not more than 12,000 tons.[2] Since the most up-to-date collieries were generally those with considerable mechanical equipment, and therefore high overhead costs, enforced reductions in output fell especially heavily on them, and made them particularly eager to buy the quotas of the less efficient firms. This happy tendency for output to be concentrated into the hands of the most modern firms was no doubt deliberately planned by the authors of this part of the scheme, though the rule of economic tender-heartedness in these matters—by which the less efficient firms are given a share in the business in order to induce the others to buy them out—has a certain Heath Robinson flavour about it, and is perhaps not the cheapest way of producing the desired result.

IRON AND STEEL

In the case of the scheme for the reorganization of the iron and steel industry, official anxiety to meet the criticism that this was just another restrictive monopoly was responsible for the association of a Government Committee with the Iron and Steel Federation (which became a price-fixing cartel for the industry) as a safeguard against any lapse into economic wickedness. When the industry was granted a $33\frac{1}{3}$ per cent tariff in 1932, the official Import Duties Advisory Committee reported that a prosperous steel industry was essential for economic progress and national security, but warned that 'the grant of protection would not suffice to place the industry in a position to play

[1] A. M. Neuman, 'Economic Organization of the British Coal Industry', London, 1934, p. 380.

[2] Op. cit., p. 435.

its proper part in the national economy unless it were accompanied by a considerable measure of reorganization '.[1] It was arranged that reorganization should proceed under the paternal eye of the Import Duties Advisory Committee itself.

In the early stages reorganization took the slightly surprising form of a further rise in the tariff to 50 per cent, which the Federation assured I.D.A.C. would not be used to raise prices. Those who noticed the curious fact that whenever prices moved at all afterwards they moved upwards must remember that there were many causes at work. Then one of the chief firms in the industry—Richard Thomas and Co.—set up a very large sheet-rolling mills at Ebbw Vale, instead of choosing the most economical location in Lincolnshire. In 1936 a syndicate outside the Federation which wanted to build a new and up-to-date steel works on the site of Palmer's Shipyard at Jarrow were spared the anxiety of risking their capital in a chancy business by the prompt efforts of Federation firms to provide the needed capacity at their own works just in time.[2] The outside syndicate broke down, and the existing firms continued to reorganize the industry themselves. In this absorbing task it was not long before they hit upon the not altogether novel expedient of a fund, financed by a levy on the whole industry, to be used in buying up and eliminating redundant plant. It is hardly necessary to add that this was called a Central Stabilization Fund.[3]

[1] 'Report of the Import Duties Advisory Committee', Cmd. 4181, 1932.

[2] 'The facts about Jarrow . . . ought to blow sky-high the strange delusions of those who believe in the "self-government of industry". . . . It is an ossification of inefficiency, an endowment of selfishness. Of the insured workers of Jarrow, 70 per cent are still unemployed', *Economist*, 18 July 1936. Cf. Ellen Wilkinson 'The Town that was Murdered', London, 1939, c. 11.

[3] Report of I.D.A.C. on 'The Present Position and Future

In the light of the enthusiastic view not unnaturally taken by I.D.A.C. of the results of the reorganization of the steel industry under its official supervision, the ill humour shown by prominent customers of the industry seems at first sight to be strangely lacking in taste. Thus the Chairman of Tube Investments, Ltd., remarked at the annual meeting of his company: 'The seriousness of to-day's position is that our foreign competitors are everywhere obtaining their steel more cheaply than we and are building up their general trade at our expense. Was it for this that the steel trade five years ago was afforded Protection? . . . In the old days the steel trade's mistakes hurt themselves only. We could buy from the foreigner if they could not produce the goods; but now that protection forces us to buy our steel at home the steel people can, and apparently do, foist the cost of their follies on the rest of the country. Was it for this that protection was afforded them?' Lord Nuffield, with characteristic bluntness, though, as Burn [1] points out, after lunch, described the Federation as 'a perfect ramp, an absolute ramp. Big cigars and nothing to do.'[2] And even the Commissioner for the Special Areas wrote, more in sorrow than in anger no doubt, that 'the advantage accruing from tariffs should be utilized to promote efficiency and ability to meet foreign competition and not merely as a

Development of the Iron and Steel Industry', Cmd. 5507, 1937, pp. 19–20.

[1] D. L. Burn, 'Economic History of Steel-Making', Cambridge, 1940, p. 495 (note).

[2] For criticism of the Federation from the Socialist camp *cf.* 'Britain Without Capitalists', by a Group of Economists, Scientists, and Technicians, London, 1936: 'Behind the whole system of linked price-fixing associations stands the British Iron and Steel Federation, which is forcing all iron and steel firms to "voluntary" association by means of interlocking agreements, rebates granted only to associated firms, and agreements between firms . . . to supply only members of associations federated into the British Iron and Steel Federation' (p. 395).

temporary shelter for making increased profits '.[1] It must be a serious disappointment for well-intentioned politicians that not even the association of an impartial Government authority with an organized industry can guarantee satisfied customers, absence of criticism in the Press, and peace and quiet in the House of Commons.

[1] Report of the Special Areas Commissioner, cited in *Economist*, 28 November 1936.

CHAPTER 3

GROWING LESS

READERS of the late nineteenth-century school of rustic romance will hardly need to be told that it is advisable to use tact with farmers. Caution has been especially necessary in this country since about 1880, when farmers began to give up on account of the growth of foreign competition, and large areas of arable land fell out of (arable) cultivation. Though there was a slow readjustment perceptible before 1914, it was not until 1931 that the Government really made amends for what was then called its long neglect, by attempting to do for farming what it was then doing for other industries. It is this tradition of half a century of neglect by authority which, though it is shared by most other industries, has been capitalized with notable success mainly by the farmers, is always liable to blunt the edge of criticism in advance, and almost makes it necessary to preface any discussion of the future of agriculture with an apology to agriculturalists.

During the half century, protests from the farmers and from their literary admirers had naturally been growing steadily in volume, and it is perhaps not out of place to mention the few economic crumbs which had come the way of the farmers in consequence. For example, by various amendments to the Finance Acts of 1887 and 1896 farmers had become entitled to alternative and advantageous methods of assessment to income tax which were not available to anyone else.[1] In 1896 agricultural land was

[1] R. S. Edwards, 'Farmers and Income Tax', *Economica*, May 1937.

exempted from 50 per cent of rates, and in 1929 let off altogether. In 1923 the Government offered loans to agricultural credit societies lending on short term, and in 1928 the Agricultural Credits Act was passed, under which a substantial Treasury grant was given to aid the formation of the Agricultural Mortgage Corporation. But in relation to what the farmers thought they ought to have got out of the Government, the proportion of these contributions seemed almost frivolous. It was perhaps inevitable that at the end of this historical period of neglect, the farmers should have seemed insatiable and the Government should have shown more haste than dignity, and certainly more charity than intelligence, in repairing its self-confessed omissions.

At any rate, in 1934 the cost of Government assistance to agriculture, according to Venn, was about £45 millions a year. In the year before the second World War, according to calculations by Sir D. Hall and the *Economist*,[1] the

[1] Sir D. Hall in 'Reconstruction and the Land', London, 1941, c. 3, gives the following estimate of State assistance to agriculture in 1938–39:

	£
Sugar beet subsidy	1,730,000
Sugar beet (remission of excise)	1,520,000
Wheat subsidy	9,290,000
Barley subsidy	800,000
Oats subsidy	2,320,000
Fat cattle subsidy	4,500,000
Milk subsidy	1,556,500
Bacon subsidy	150,000
Land fertility scheme	1,300,000
Ploughing up subsidy	500,000
Drainage	400,000
Livestock improvement	100,000
Rating relief	17,000,000
Total	£41,166,500

To this the *Economist* (10 January 1942) adds £60 millions, which, farmers were allowing themselves to accept a little over £100 millions from the community without a blush.

The absence of the latter may perhaps be explained by the fact that some of the money reached the farmers indirectly and with its public origin disguised. Thus some agrarian embarrassment may have been saved because the sugar-beet subsidy was canalized through the sugar-beet companies, who, as one of their directors jocularly admitted, 'shared the swag' with the farmers afterwards.[1] There seems some ground for thinking that the sugar companies could well afford to share it,[2] though it is a little mystifying to learn that such opulence could be founded on a crop which, according to the Greene Committee,[3] would in 1935 have been completely valueless without the subsidy. Actually, State assistance in this case before the war was about equal in amount to farmers' receipts before deduction of the cost of transport. It would therefore have profited the country, and left the farmers equally satisfied, if the beets had been ploughed into the earth again or fed to cattle free.

---

according to Sir D. Hall, was the extra cost of obtaining the British agricultural output at home over what it would have cost if bought abroad.

[1] An expression favoured by Sir George Courthope, a director of several sugar factories, in a Parliamentary debate on 10 February 1936.

[2] By 1936 the beet-sugar companies had repaid 18½ per cent of their capital, had accumulated assets equal to nearly 27 per cent of their remaining capital, had written off 42 per cent of their expenditure on fixed assets, and had repaid gross dividends amounting to more than 83 per cent of the share capital outstanding. *Economist*, 8 February 1936.

[3] The Greene Committee proposed to abolish the subsidy because there was 'no positive justification for the expenditure of a sum of several millions per annum on an industry which has no reasonable prospect of ever becoming self-supporting, and on the production of a crop which, without that assistance, would, at present sugar prices, be practically valueless'. Cmd 4871, 1935, p. 102.

The wheat subsidy similarly was not a direct charge on the Exchequer, but was financed by a levy on flour importers and millers. It was also not a net gain to wheat-farmers who had formerly fed much of their product to livestock, and were now obliged to buy imported feeding-stuffs instead, and on a rising market. Some agrarian qualms of conscience may perhaps have been quieted by the thought that iniquity out of which one makes so little profit does not count. But from the point of view of the consumer this consideration cannot abate the injustice of a tax on bread, which is what the wheat levy amounted to.

The reason why subsidies fell out of favour may have had something to do with the fact that they are normally voted annually, and therefore come under periodical public scrutiny, with all the risks which experience (notably in 1921, when the Corn Production subsidies were swept away at short notice) shows that that implies. No doubt also a good many farmers must have found the odd situation of 'an industry only held up by protection and subsidies, though the richest market in the world is at its doors',[1] rather suggestive. Whatever the reason, the grand assault on this market opened after 1933 with a new and far stronger weapon.

The characteristic and most important form of Government assistance to the farmers before the war was neither direct nor indirect subsidies, but statutory marketing schemes, set up under the Agricultural Marketing Act of 1933 and protected by import quotas.

A statutory Marketing Scheme has been described as a sort of Fairyland for good farmers,[2] where the weather

[1] Sir D. Hall in 'Reconstruction and the Land', London, 1941, p. 63.

[2] The State 'handing him the keys wherewith to open, if he will, the palace called Organized Marketing, where the enchanted princess, disguised as the British housewife, awaits him'. From the Presidential address of J. M. Caie delivered to Section M of the British Association for the Advancement of Science, September 1937.

ceases from troubling and the foreign exporter is at rest. It is not surprising to learn that the economic life of Fairyland is based, broadly speaking, on the agreeable principle that the less the fortunate inhabitants produce, the more they get paid for it. As in the real world, there is a reward for good farmers, though the others may be forgiven for reflecting thankfully that the resemblance ends there. In Fairyland there is no penalty for *bad* farmers, because the efficient ones get paid too much in order that the inefficient ones may get a living. Ultimately, it is to be feared, certain alien elements in Fairyland—namely, landlords—get what would be called in the United States a handsome rake-off from the increased earnings of good and bad farmers alike, through higher rents. But this result, though unintentional, comes about only after long delays.

The machinery of a Marketing Scheme is set up when a majority of the producers concerned vote in favour of it, when it becomes mandatory on the minority if it is approved by the Government. Non-co-operative behaviour by the minority afterwards, such as price-cutting, is apt to be costly to them, since the Boards normally have, and use, the power to fine recalcitrant members.[1] The prime object of the Scheme is to restrict sales, and thus bring about a higher price, which is protected against foreign exporters by a quota on imports. Many observers point out that it is this restriction on foreign imports which is the *sine qua non* of orderly marketing; and it must be admitted that in some cases in practice, once imports are cut down by a quota, there is a noticeable loss of interest by the farmers in any further proceedings.

With the pronounced success of the first schemes, the general tendency has been for farmers to change to the cultivation of the favoured products where they can, and

[1] Cf. 'Report of the Departmental Committee on the Infliction of Penalties by Agricultural Marketing Boards', Cmd. 5980, April 1939.

where they cannot for the scope of the schemes to be extended to new products. It is curious that by 1939 no further progress had been made in this direction than a Board apiece for Pigs, Hops, Bacon, Milk and Potatoes. The contributor to a learned journal, who, in a study of a much-neglected branch of the farming business, suggested a Bed-and-Breakfast Marketing Board,[1] was undeniably far in advance of his age and generation. But there seems no doubt that he diagnosed the general drift of affairs correctly enough.

With the extension of marketing schemes to new products, various practical problems came to the fore which were different from those encountered in the analogous but less disguised forms of restrictionism in industry, and since 1933 constant experimentation has evolved a group of principles which may not unfairly be described as Economic Wrinkles or Rules of Thumb in Orderly Marketing. The development of these rules is of interest from the point of view of the light it throws on the basic object of these schemes.

MILK

The hallmark of success in orderly marketing is clearly the attraction exercised on new producers to enter the market; the consequential problem is how to dispose of the increased aggregate production without disappointing all the producers by a fall in price. The key to this problem is to be found in the well-known economic truth that if a monopolistic seller can charge different people different prices for the same thing he will make more money than if he charges everybody the same.[2] This truth seems to

[1] *Economist*, 19 September 1936.

[2] Provided that the elasticities of demand in the separate markets are not equal—a condition which in practice is almost always fulfilled. Cf. Joan Robinson, 'Economics of Imperfect Competition', London, 1934, p. 181.

have been realized earlier and taken to heart more seriously by the English Milk Marketing Board than by any other group of producers. As production increased the Board offered milk at specially low prices for manufacture into a series of various useful articles, ranging from cheese to umbrella handles; when surpluses became alarming, it offered the same milk to school-children at a halfpenny a glass which cost anyone else a penny and cost umbrella manufacturers half a farthing. The novitiate in these matters might have supposed that the Board would have justified its policy of charging different people different prices for the same thing by explaining how much lower the price of milk for the ordinary consumer could be fixed if the surplus which might otherwise be wasted was sold to umbrella-makers and similar deserving folk for use in manufacture. But those in authority showed a certain coyness about reducing prices to the ordinary consumer. The retail price rose, in fact, about 10 per cent from 1933 to 1937, in the first four years of the Board's existence.[1] However, with more and more farmers getting to know about the advantages of orderly marketing in milk, the 'surplus' for manufacture increased so substantially that the price of milk for *manufacture* had to be reduced. Even the most fervent supporters of the Scheme could hardly deny that there was an element of the unexpected in a situation where those who drank milk paid more for it, while those who preferred it in umbrella handles paid less. And a certain bewilderment, not unmixed with suspicion that the Board was serving primarily the producers' interest, became general when the official spokesmen, precluded from

[1] 'Annual Report of the Food Council 1938–9', quoted in 'The Agricultural Register 1938–9', Oxford, 1939, p. 126. At one time the price of milk was rising when the price of all other foods was falling. The index is shown in Ashby and Jones, 'The Milk Industry' ('Britain in Recovery', London, 1938).

explaining that milk to drink was cheap because the surplus was manufactured, explained that milk to drink was dear because it was essential that milk for manufacture should be cheap![1] As all this time the Board's posters (partly financed by the Treasury) were exhorting people to 'Drink More Milk' (whatever the price), an attitude of pained surprise on the part of the ordinary citizen at these proceedings might well have seemed appropriate.

In 1934 the rising tide of milk production threatened to swamp the umbrella trade and other manufacturers on whom the stream had been diverted in order to maintain an orderly (and profitable) market for milk to drink. Cows began to be seen by bemused travellers in all sorts of unlikely places, and particularly in places remote from any convenient market.[2] So in order to keep up the spirits of farmers producing for the manufacturing end of the business, the Board, after toying with the idea of production quotas, finally got the Government to guarantee a standard minimum price for manufactured milk somewhat above the then ruling price, on condition of repayment if the ruling price subsequently rose above the minimum.[3] In default of this subsidy the average returns of all producers (which were made to vary with the price of both liquid and manufacturing milk) would have fallen, and inefficient and badly situated farmers would have been forced out of production. Perhaps

[1] 'To justify an increase in the price of milk for babies by the low price for umbrella handles is the economics of Bedlam.' *Economist*, 7 August 1937.

[2] The regional price policy adopted gave a particular stimulus to production in the regions farthest from the markets. Cf. Sorenson and Cassels 'The English Milk Market' in *Quarterly Journal of Economics*, February 1936.

[3] The ruling price did so rise, but, due to various misunderstandings, 'in actual fact the Boards did not repay any of the money advanced to them to raise the price of manufacturing milk', 'Trade Regulations and Commercial Policy of U.K.', National Institute of Social and Economic Research, London, 1941.

the spectacle of the public Treasury handing out public money which 'becomes in effect a subsidy to maintain a high price to the public and to hinder the transfer of the trade to the cheapest producers'[1] is best regarded as light relief in an otherwise complicated situation. It remains to add that the Board was careful to secure that no foreign umbrella manufacturer should be able to undersell the home producer if the price of manufacturing milk rose too fast. Quotas were applied on imports of condensed milk, powder, and cream.

It seems clear that the Milk Marketing Board can have had little ground for complaint against Government Departments, which, from the Treasury, the Board of Trade, and the Ministry of Agriculture downwards, rallied loyally to its assistance in a most gratifying way. By 1939, however, despite all possible official help, the Board could hardly help becoming aware of a hint of criticism from various quarters. The price of milk to drink was thought so high that even the milk distributors protested on behalf of the public until they were pacified by an increase in their margins. And the price of manufacturing milk, under constant pressure from an increasing volume of supply, got lower and lower, until there was practically no sale for skim. In July 1939 the Brighton Sewers Board gave permission to a Hove dairy to discharge 1,500 gallons of skim milk daily for about a month into the river.[2] These events provided a rather odd climax for a regime of orderly marketing, and in order to disarm suspicion that they were due to the policy of the Board in serving too exclusively the interests of the producers, the Government proposed to set up an official advisory body called the Milk Commission, consisting of nine persons with no financial interest in the business. It is understandable, however, that the producers felt a certain resentment at the implication of

[1] Sir D. Hall, op. cit., p. 236.
[2] *The Times*, 29 July 1939.

reproach in this proposal, and after an embarrassing interlude, harmony was restored when the Milk Commission scheme was withdrawn and a new Bill on more familiar lines, including subsidy and price insurance provisions for butter and cheese, was introduced instead.

POTATOES

After the diverting, if not dramatic perplexities of milk marketing, the other marketing schemes seem rather humdrum. But they have had their practical problems too. In the case of potatoes, for example, it was obvious from the start that if the scheme was too successful, everybody might decide to grow potatoes, even the humblest window-box contributing its earthy quota. Faced with these frightening possibilities, the Potato Marketing Board hit on the idea of registering all the people who happened to be potato-growers in 1934 and fining those who wanted to come into the business for the first time £5 an acre. The product was then put through a sieve, and by varying the mesh the Board could penalize unco-operative producers who grew potatoes of the wrong size,[1] and so improve the returns of the others. Rejects could be fed to cattle or sold for manufacture at a low price on the model of the Milk Board's policy of discriminating monopoly already described. If on account of weather conditions there were large variations in the crop, variable quotas on imports could be used to throw the risk of price movements on to the foreign exporter.

From the home producer's point of view this was an eminently satisfactory arrangement, and it is perhaps not unlikely that some of them may have asked themselves occasionally whether Nature had not invented the homely tuber with the problems of orderly marketing in mind.

[1] Cf. the charges made against potato-growers for 'growing potatoes of the wrong size' in *Manchester Guardian*, 30 January 1939.

HOPS

Hops, however, proved an even better raw material. The Hops Marketing Scheme imposed a complete ban on any new producers whatever, and formed those who happened to be growing hops between 1928 and 1932 into a tight monopoly. Prices were fixed in advance for a period of five years by a friendly arrangement between the Board and the brewers' association, also a monopoly, and foreign imports were subjected to high duties and to quantitative limitation. The success of this scheme was immediate and total.

PIGS

Pigs, on the other hand, must have seemed to the innocent and ingenious experts of the Ministry of Agriculture as though they had been sent to try us. They cannot easily be put through sieves or other forms of treatment for standardization, they have alternative uses—for bacon and pork—and about four-fifths of the British requirements of bacon were normally filled by import from abroad. The Reorganization Commission appointed by the Government did not hesitate long over this last problem—they concluded that no clearer reason could be given for the expansion of the bacon industry at home than the importation of large quantities of bacon from abroad,[1] and two Marketing Boards were accordingly set up with this line of thought in mind. The other difficulties proved more troublesome.

With the object of making the Scheme go with a bang from the start, pig prices were fixed so as to cover feeding-stuff and other costs, whatever they might be. Unfortunately the bacon factories found it impossible to sell bacon at these prices, and the pig producers made heavy losses, from which they were barely rescued when the

[1] 'Report of Reorganization Commission for Pigs' (Ministry of Agriculture Economic Series, No. 38), pp. 17–18.

Treasury rushed into the breach with a loan of £160,000. Thereafter, pig producers were a little backward in providing supplies for the factories, preferring to supply the pork market instead, and a situation of some piquancy arose in which bacon imports were being drastically restricted by a quota imposed in order to protect a marketing scheme which the producers themselves failed to support. But the Treasury again rose to the occasion, and this time, under the Bacon Industry Act of 1938, subsidized the producers when their costs rose above a certain normal figure.[1] An authority was also set up to restrict the production of bacon by a licensing scheme and given the somewhat unexpected name of the Bacon Development Board; and the all-important quota was reorganized. At first the quota was applied against former important suppliers, fixed very low, and made liable to adjustment monthly—in practice usually downwards. But the wily Danes evaded it, sending their bacon to this country via Germany, which was not an 'important supplier'. The prohibition of 'the importation of any bacon produced in a foreign country from pigs bred in any other foreign country'[2] stopped this leak.

Although the factories and farms in the industry have had their ups and downs, and in 1939 still felt a sense of grievance against the Government for its miserliness,[3] it seemed clear

[1] The Act provided a price formula, according to which the price of bacon pigs was fixed in proportion to the cost of the standard feeding ration. If the cost of this ration, as ascertained by the Ministry of Agriculture, moved above 8*s.* 6*d.*, the Treasury provided a subsidy which was paid to curers and passed on by them to producers.

[2] S.R.O. 1935, 1237.

[3] Cf. statement of Mr. Holdsworth in the House of Commons Debate on the Bacon Industry Bill, 11 April 1938: 'It is an astonishing thing, with all the help that agriculture is getting from the House, that agricultural members are still complaining of the inadequacy of the gifts extended to them'.

that the devotion of the Treasury to their cause could ultimately be counted on to save them in emergency.[1] The bacon consumer no doubt found it a little odd that home-produced bacon cost more and imported bacon very much more than before, particularly in view of the trouble taken to 'rationalize' the home industry. The Danes also found it a little unexpected that their returns on selling a smaller quantity of bacon to this country at a very high price were greater than when a much larger quantity was sold here at a lower price, and might have wondered why so much trouble was taken by the Government of their principal customers to bring about a situation so clearly unfavourable to the latter. An attitude of philosophical tolerance in face of the peculiar preferences of the inscrutable island race no doubt seemed proper to them at that time and in keeping with the high price of their product in England.

Before the outbreak of war it appeared that the farmers were at last beginning to see reason and acknowledge that orderly marketing was not the hollow and unsubstantial political promise which they had feared at first. It is true that there were some fretful and discordant voices, such as the gloomy *Economist*, which in the year before the war said, 'We drift from Bill to Bill, creating by a process of economic casuistry one vested interest after another. . . . We are within measureable distance of setting up a new feudal system, with the British market instead of the British land, parcelled out among the barons'.[2] But perhaps this criticism was not intended too seriously, as the journal was completely answered by one of its contributors, who, in a study of the Cornish broccoli industry, where the

[1] New subsidies for the Bacon Marketing Board were being suggested just before the war. E.g., Sir A. Gridley proposed a Treasury advance of £750,000 in July 1939.

[2] 2 April 1938.

growers got protection equivalent to £25 an acre, pointed out that this protection was granted only because certain wily foreigners, wedged between us and the Equator, have for decades been taking surreptitious advantage of the earlier ripening of their vegetation. This seems to go to the heart of all agrarian grievances in this country. How much better, wrote this contributor, if the British Isles were at the North Pole instead of in their present dangerous position so near to the broccoli-growing foreigner! Clearly, very much better indeed, and not only for the Cornish broccoli-grower; though perhaps not without drawbacks for the rest of us.

CHAPTER 4

WORKING LESS

'ALL classes of society are trade unionists at heart', wrote Jevons in 1882,[1] 'and differ chiefly in the boldness, ability and secrecy with which they push their respective interests.' This statement commends itself to common sense as not without a certain resemblance to the truth; and will make it unnecessary in what follows to refer often to the fact that what certain groups have been known to do in their own interest other groups would like to do but cannot, and still others have already been doing for generations but have not yet been found out.

The practice amongst workers of all types of forming fraternal associations in order to maintain and improve their material conditions is not a modern one. It was about the eleventh century, according to Carr Saunders and Wilson,[2] when 'a great movement towards association began to sweep like a wave over the cities of Europe'; and it seems not inappropriate that amongst the first exclusive, professional groups to be formed were those of university professors, shortly before A.D. 1200. Numerous gilds of medieval traders and craftsmen were, however, already in existence at this date, so that it is therefore justifiable to describe the principle of exclusive association amongst working men as extremely ancient and respectable.

In modern times, the means by which workers' groups bring about improvements in their economic position are not essentially dissimilar from the means employed by

[1] W. S. Jevons, 'The State in Relation to Labour', London, 1882.

[2] 'The Professions', Carr Saunders and Wilson, Oxford, 1933, p. 289.

associations of business men to the same end. Modern developments of capitalistic technique have, however, placed in the hands of the workers a powerful weapon quite unknown to business practice—namely, the strike—by which at some chosen moment they can refuse to work at all except under conditions laid down by themselves. It is presumably the disagreeable associations with the use of this weapon in the nineteenth century which led Dr. Arnold to deny that Trade Unions were respectable at all and to describe them as 'fearful engines of mischief, ready to riot and assassinate'.

In these days it is sometimes a little difficult to see a group of workers on strike as a fearful engine of mischief, particularly if the dispute is about some obscure and technical aspect of their trade—as, for example, the strike of the caddies in Providence, Rhode Island, for permission to use the municipal golf course themselves free of charge on Mondays.[1] Moreover, the use of the strike weapon is no longer confined to Trade Unions of manual workers, but is now spreading to the most dignified and respectable professional bodies. Thus, in recent times, a body no less eminent than the professors and assistant professors of the University of Teheran struck work because 'the authorities had not made proper use of the educated classes in the matter of appointments to the Ministry of Education'.[2] And something very much like a strike of the British medical profession occurred in 1911, when 26,000 practitioners were called on by the British Medical Association to refuse service under the National Health Insurance Act.

The strike weapon has been known and gradually perfected over a century or more, and it is now accepted as a normal incident of industrial life. Apart from the dilemma of the sympathetic strike, of which more here-

[1] 'Strikes of Government Employees', D. Ziskind, New York, 1940, p. 98.

[2] *Journal de Tehran*, 5 April 1943.

after, it has raised few problems in the inter-war period which have not been discussed at length before. A far less dramatic, more insidious, and from the point of view of economic progress, perhaps more important development, is the tendency of unorganized groups of workers to go slow to protect their jobs [1] and the tendency of organized groups of workers to restrict their output by various industrial practices which can be operated, not like strikes, for relatively short periods at relatively long intervals of time, but continuously and indefinitely. These practices became of special importance in the inter-war period. They are perhaps best described in the order in which they might be expected to occur to an enterprising Trade Union official bent on serving the interests of his constituents.

The first and perhaps the easiest move in the direction of labour restriction is merely to refrain from bringing the terms of previous contracts with employers up to date. The wages of spinners in the cotton industry, for example, are in some places based on piece-work lists which were drawn up in 1860, when the conditions of work were a little different and on the whole a little more arduous than at present. A more positive practice is for the Union to condone or to encourage a natural human disposition to go slow, and to penalize those of the unnatural minority who go fast. Hence the rules of the Engineering Union, which provided that members doing more than ' a reasonable day's work ' should be fined a pound; and hence the story of what would now be called the Stakhanovite of the riveting industry, who earned three times the standard rate because he was especially good at the job, and was subsequently fined and dismissed from the Union on this account.[2]

[1] Cf. ' The Man on the Job ', *Planning*, April 1945, and references therein to the pioneer work of Vernon, Sargant Florence, Mathewson, and others.

[2] Unless otherwise stated, the examples of restrictive practices in this chapter refer to the pre-1939 period and are taken from ' Are

The most obvious and most popular restrictive strategy, however, is to follow the line so clearly laid down by associations of business men, and restrict entry to the trade. Most Trade Unions of skilled or semi-skilled workers—to judge from their sometimes open hostility to Government training schemes for ex-service and unemployed men in the inter-war period—seem to feel rather strongly that new-comers to their respective trades would do better somewhere else. Though if all took this view it is plain that there would have to be a Union of Residuals, based on the model which made such a promising start in Mexico City recently,[1] and consisting of those who could not get into any other Union.

Following successful business practice, the admission to a trade may be restricted by imposing the irrelevant qualification of sex, women being explicitly debarred, for instance, from certain branches of boot and shoe manufacture and flour-milling, and implicitly debarred from very many other industries and professions; or it may be based on the fortunate accident of membership of the group, as when Unions in the printing trades and certain branches of the textile and building trades got the employers to agree to the principle of the 'closed shop', according to which only their members and no outsiders should be employed [2];

Trade Unions Obstructive?—An Impartial Enquiry', John Hilton and Others, London, 1935, and the Ministry of Labour Enquiry into Apprenticeship and Training 1925–6 (7 vols.).

[1] 'Mexico City beggars, stating that they wanted an eight-hour day and better working conditions, sought to register a union, but the authorities refused their application.' *News Chronicle*, 3 December 1937. It is a sobering thought that Residuals will probably not even be allowed to become film artists. The Westminster Industrial Court recommended recently that 'crowd' workers must become members of the Film Artists Association and only those actually deriving a living from 'crowd' scenes should continue in the industry. *The Times*, 30 January 1945.

[2] These agreements are sometimes strengthened by the mono-

or it may be based on the irrelevant accident that the member happened to be working in the trade on some previous date. The Government itself endorsed this well-established principle in the Mining Industry Act of 1926, which empowers the Minister of Labour to regulate entry to the industry so that preference is given to those employed in it before 30 April 1926.[1] The commonest method of restricting entry, however, is to limit the number of apprentices to a trade and leave employers to select the best themselves. This causes a scarcity of labour in due course, which strengthens the bargaining position of the Union and improves the economic prospects of its members, especially if the apprenticeship period can be made to last several years. In many trades the normal apprenticeship period is seven years, which contrasts somewhat oddly with the seven years required for a full-scale medical training and the few months required (in war-time) to train expert aircraft mechanics. At any rate, the strict limitation of the number of apprentices per skilled worker in the furniture and printing trades seems to have improved the position of the older workers considerably, though, according to some critics, at the expense of the young entrant to industry in general and of the future of the specified trade in particular. As a Trade Union official in the cotton trade remarked in an unguarded moment during the Hilton enquiry, 'I always regard apprenticeship as a means of keeping out adults

---

polistic union agreeing not to allow its members to work for any employers not members of the monopolistic Trade Association. This gives both parties a common stake in restrictionism. Thus in one case quoted by PEP (*Planning*, May 1944) 'the scope and strength of the Federation is very materially assisted by the pressure brought to bear upon non-federated firms by the Union. There is a very clear and definite mutual understanding between the Federation and the Union upon this point.'

[1] Section 18 of the Mining Industry Act of 1926.

who might come in and learn the trade in two or three weeks' !

A more diplomatically minded official, better acquainted with the text-books, might have explained that the apprenticeship system is necessary to guarantee high standards of craftsmanship, without which the trade's obligation of loyal service to the public could not be properly fulfilled. Though even a Talleyrand amongst trade unionists could not deny that in some trades the apprenticeship period is so long, the entry so small, and the task of the apprentices so pedestrian that the cloven hoof of restrictionism for the sake of those already in the trade is glaringly obvious. When this is explained, however, the characteristic reaction of the reformers is to conclude that the obvious policy in this matter must be the wrong one. They do not, that is to say, conclude that standards of craftsmanship need only be as high as the consuming public requires: they discover that the setting of standards should be undertaken for *all* trades generally and is a task which can only be adequately performed by the Government.

Demarcation rules, restricting particular jobs to particular trades, are a more subtle but no less effective way of safeguarding the interest of a skilled trade or section of a trade, and in many cases they are a necessary complement of restricted entry, which would otherwise cause employers to substitute the commoner skills for the scarce ones—e.g., hot-water fitters for plumbers, bricklayers for plasterers, and other monstrous anomalies too horrible to describe. The rules come most frequently to public attention in the building trade. Every housewife knows that to fix a wash-hand basin requires a bricklayer to put up the brackets, a plumber to fix the basin, and a hot-water fitter to bring the hot-water pipes to the floor level (but not above); or that to fix a door, a bricklayer is needed to knock a hole in the wall, a joiner to fit the door, a plasterer to make good the damage done by the bricklayer, and a painter to make good the damage done by everybody to the paintwork. Even those not in contact with domestic realities, however, may guess that similar restrictions are common in many other industries besides building.

In the engineering industry, for example, exactly similar pipes must be handled by different trades, according to whether they are on a building or a ship. On board the ship, ' drains ' are the province of one trade, ' scuppers ' of another. Where electrical work is involved, the division of jobs between engineers and electricians is complex indeed, as is clear from the story of the electro-mechanical brake.[1]

> ' Four men were appointed to the job—a fitter and his mate, and an electrician and his mate. The last-mentioned pair started first, and disconnected the wires conveying current. Then the fitter and his mate removed the nuts and lifted off the iron cover. The electrician and his mate then withdrew the electric magnet coil. Then the fitter and his mate proceeded to remove other nuts, pins, springs, etc., and readjusted the tension on the mechanical parts of the brake. This being done, all the former operations were repeated in backward order, until the job was completed. Each pair of men had their own kit of tools, which had to be spread out each time an operation was performed, and removed so as to enable the next pair of men to act similarly.'

In the printing industry, which has been very highly mechanized, the rigidity of labour restrictions is in proportion to the strength of the Unions. Thus, machine-minders are forbidden by Trade Union rule to make any alterations in type, however trivial. These must be made

[1] John Hilton, op. cit., p. 148.

by compositors. Boys set to sweep the floor must not touch bales of paper, as the handling of these is a preserve of the Paper-workers' Union. London newspapers each have to have a separate staff, even if morning and evening newspapers are produced by the same concern in the same building.

No doubt the more impracticable demarcation rules are more honoured in the breach than in the observance, and some of the others can be justified by technical reasons; that is, in the absence of the rules, employers would themselves refrain from substituting unsuitable skills in the interest of the efficiency of production. But not all. A certain embarrassment on this subject is discernible in the Union rule according to which members can be fined for 'instructing any one not connected with our society (except legal apprentices) by allowing him to practise with his tools'. And in the case of some practices specifically excluding women, such as the bar in the London furniture trades against women upholstering furniture, the pretence that only the insiders can do the job is thinner still. *Local* demarcations, such as that which prevents the transfer of dockers from one wharf to another of the same concern if the volume of work requires it, or that which bars provincial compositors from getting a job in the same line of work in London, seem to the uninitiated to be nothing but a means of creating an artificial scarcity of labour for the benefit of groups of workers which happen to be particularly well organized, and at the expense of the others. But no doubt the technical complexities of particular trades are a trap for the unwary, and no broad generalization of this kind would commend itself to the experts engaged in them.

Whether the suspicions of the ignorant are well-founded or not, it would be impossible to deny that different views can be held in the same industry about demarcation rules, and in fact the harmony of the industrial scene is often unhappily marred by disputes about them. Employers frequently disagree with Unions about who is to do what, and a strike sometimes becomes necessary to discover the right solution. Unions frequently disagree with one another on the same issue, and both may go on strike against the same employer because this is their only means of indicating their disapproval of each other. Unfortunately, when the trial of strength comes, the Press reports are generally quite incomprehensible to the general public, which cannot understand why five hundred engineers should stop work because a man demonstrating a gear-cutting machine puts on an overall, or that a strike should occur because two Unions cannot agree whether shipwrights or joiners should make wooden moulds for a concrete dock. More unfortunately still, even when these obscure mysteries have been cleared up to the satisfaction of the parties immediately concerned, some nuisance is sure to discover new and better ways of doing an old job or invent new jobs for making new products altogether, and at once the seed is sown of fresh disputes. The worn-out negotiators on both sides may well feel that economic progress is a standing threat to industrial peace and that it ought to be abolished. When it was decided to try the experiment of putting tiles instead of cement on a theatre floor, for instance,[1] the plasterers stopped work because the bricklayers were put on to the tiling, and the bricklayers did the same when the plasterers were given the job. When—as a desperate remedy of last resort—it was finally decided to entrust the tilers with the laying of the tiles and everybody stopped work, the parties concerned must have felt this behaviour not altogether inappropriate in a topsy-turvy world where tiles are put to such peculiar uses.

Sometimes the new jobs are merely more highly mechanized versions of the old ones and can be done with

[1] Hilton, op. cit., p. 22.

less effort. This leads to disputes of the more-looms-per-weaver, less-men-per-crane and less-men-per-printing-press variety, where the not uncommon attitude of the Unions is that if mechanical improvements are introduced, the earnings of the skilled man deprived of his job thereby should be a permanent charge on the undertaking, though the work required may have been degraded to mere machine-minding. The implications of such a view, if it had been consistently and successfully adopted throughout the last hundred years, open up many interesting trains of thought.

Although the victory in disputes about demarcation and other restrictive practices may seem to go to one side or the other without much reference to the technical considerations in each case, certain marked and not always reassuring tendencies obtrude. The first is that success depends not so much on the merits of the case as on the bargaining strength behind it. In times of good trade and a sellers' market, restrictive practices multiply and are enforced; in a slump they can be overridden. The second is that in the sheltered trades, safeguarded by some form of natural or statutory protection, disputes over restrictive practices (though not the practices themselves) are apt to be few and relations between Trade Unions and Trade Associations very harmonious.[1] More important in the long run is the noticeable tendency of the employer who feels hard pressed

[1] The railways are a good case. But no doubt there is a general tendency for complementary monopolies to hang together lest they should hang separately. Thus the railway Unions have publicly intervened in the road *v.* rail controversy on the side of their employers. Their members who happen to be members of Local Authority finance committees also customarily press the railways' case in local rating disputes. In the iron and steel industry the Trade Unions are as protectionist as their employers. The Iron and Steel Trades Confederation recommends in its post-war plans the 'replacement of at least 2 million tons of imported iron and steel products'. *The Times*, 25 June 1945.

by these restrictions and can modify his product slightly without spoiling the market, to substitute new processes and materials for scarce skilled labour. Thus machine-made plaster boards can displace plasterers altogether for certain types of work, artificial stone, which is set by brick-layers, can displace stone-masons, and wood can displace tilers for internal work. Ultimately the industry itself may show signs of migrating to another part of the country or to another country altogether, where the restrictions are less onerous. There was some evidence of the latter tendency in shipbuilding before the war.

Prominent business men from time to time work themselves into a fine frenzy of indignation over labour restrictions. But their oratory is not always free from a hint of the pot calling the kettle black. There is even an element of rough justice in a system under which the poor, who are the chief sufferers from restrictionism, use against their employers and the general public the identical weapons from which the latter suffer so much at the hands of the former. But it will always be difficult for the man in the street to understand why working less should increase the general welfare. Not many of the uninitiated can expect to understand fully the refined and subtle methods of restrictionism practised by business men; but few indeed of the general public, dwelling perhaps for ever in the uttermost confines of heathen economic darkness, will be brought to believe that society will be one whit better off if the butcher works less, the baker restricts the number of his apprentices to protect his old age, and the candlestick maker insists on doing everything by hand. Even in economic matters there are limits to the credulity of the Common Man. The misfortune is that indignation on the subject is not aroused by *all* restrictive practices, whether overt or disguised, and whether applied by workers' interests or any other interests in society.

CHAPTER 5

TRANSPORTING LESS

THE five plumbers who in 1939 were fined for travelling to work in a car 'in direct competition with the public service system'[1] might have been forgiven if they had described the transport industry as being organized by Parliamentary Private Bill Committees, the Railway Rates Tribunal, three Railway and Canal Commissioners, thirty-four Traffic Commissioners, the Board of Trade, and the Ministry of Transport, in the interests of the railway and road transport companies then in the business and with the object of keeping new-comers out. Such a lapse from the strict truth, though pardonable perhaps in plumbers, would certainly have been deplored in serious students of the subject, and particularly by those in the industry. But as an expository device for drawing attention to certain broad features of the situation, the judgement would have had some point.

The largest old-established firms in the inland transport industry are the railway companies, whose strictly regulated but not uncomfortable position as a sort of collective monopoly controlled by Parliament began to be threatened after the last war by the incursion of road transport undertakings. The first public reaction to this development resembled a vague feeling of sympathy for an aged and well-disciplined servant who cannot manage the stairs in the new house as well as his juniors. There might have been some advantage in inquiring whether the very severe discipline in the old nineteenth-century house (particularly in the

[1] *The Times*, 17 May 1939.

matter of railway rates) was altogether appropriate to the new one of the period after 1918. No doubt such an inquiry would have led to some very drastic changes, particularly in rates as between one place and another and one trader and another, and many business relationships built up over long periods on the basis of railway rates fixed absolutely or fixed in relation to other rates would have been disturbed,[1] to the accompaniment of loud protests from the important and well-established interests affected. The Government can hardly be blamed for preferring the less heroic and at the same time more fashionable course. Instead of relaxing the out-of-date statutory restrictions on railway companies in order to put competition between them and the road undertakings on a fair basis, they imposed restrictions on road undertakings.

If the object had been to maintain the value of railway stock against further depreciation, there was, no doubt, a good deal to be said for this course. And although the view implicitly held by some protagonists of the railways' case, that most railway stockholders are widows or orphans, must be accepted with a grain of salt, good reasons can be found for the protection of the types of railway stock largely held by trustees. At the same time, a captious critic might have pointed out that the method actually adopted tended to maintain the value of railway *equipment* as it was then, whereas a relaxation of restrictions would have forced substantial re-equipment to meet road competition. No traveller with experience of railway facilities and railway rates in the United States and some continental countries could maintain that Britain led the world in these respects. And no economist could deny that there are circumstances in which railway lines however well built, waiting-rooms however cosy, and crossing gates however picturesque,

[1] Cf. Gilbert Walker, 'Road and Rail', London, 1942, p. 134.

must be simply abandoned under penalty of continuous losses.[1]

From the time when the first railway managers fought their Bills through Parliament against the vested interests of landowners, canal owners and stage-coach undertakings, until the present, the railways have had a long and intensive experience of statutory controls of one kind or another. Perhaps it was with the idea of drawing on this experience that the curious policy was adopted of associating the railways with the official machinery for fixing road passenger fares. At any rate, the rather surprising consequence has been that road operators have not been allowed in practice to reduce their fares merely because the railways have reduced theirs [2]—a policy which may also have helped to maintain the value of railway stock.

The method of imposing controls on the road transport business has been to restrict entry to it by means of a licensing system under the Road Traffic Act of 1930 and the Road and Rail Traffic Act of 1933. The provisions of these Acts governing the issue of licences are not remarkable for clarity, though it does appear that the draftsmen were fully seized of the disastrous consequences (for the licensees, not the public) of transport services being provided 'in excess of requirements'—a contingency which the Act of 1933 *obliges* the licensing authority to take into account.[3] A satisfactory understanding of the conditions of issue can only come from some knowledge of the way they have been hammered out in practice.

Foremost amongst these conditions is one which is not unfamiliar in other industrial contexts—namely, that of a

[1] Cf. Ponsonby, 'An Aspect of Competition in Transport', *Economica*, November 1935.

[2] D. N. Chester, 'Public Control of Road Passenger Transport', Manchester, 1936, p. 171.

[3] Road and Rail Traffic Act of 1933, Part 1, Section 6 (2).

certain regard for the interests of the old-established firms in the business. It is perhaps unavoidable that this principle should not commend itself to compressed and harassed motor-coach passengers at excursion times for example, though a public-spirited minority amongst them could perhaps after a struggle be got to appreciate the argument that if new-comers were not excluded they would add to traffic congestion. There were, indeed, certain incorrigible grumblers who insisted that traffic congestion was caused by the parking of private cars in the streets, and not by motor-coaches at all, but they seldom found it worth while to try to catch the ear of the Traffic Commissioner. If the old-established firm happened to be the local council, which operated trams, many of which had, no doubt, given half a century's unbroken service to the relief of the rates, the argument that trams are quieter and quicker than any bus service owned by interlopers who take money out of the town could be made to sound impressive to the rate-payers at least.

But it is clear that these arguments cannot always be relied on to convince the majority, particularly if the new-comer is insistent and offers much cheaper fares. In practice a good deal of reliance was placed in the discouraging aspect of the mere number of objectors to a new scheme, as in the case of the small bus-owner in Glasgow who thought he might like to run some tours. On appeal, he was opposed by two Local Authorities, two railway companies, five associated bus companies, and one independent.[1] He decided not to. If, finally, the worst comes to the worst, and new services have to be provided because the existing services are inadequate, the old-established firms can be given the first chance of providing it.[2]

[1] A. R. Fairburn, R.V.A. 2941, January 1935, quoted Chester, op. cit., p. 183.

[2] Cf. Chester, op. cit., p. 198.

The principle of tenderness towards the old firms—in this case those who were lucky enough to be operating in 1933—is also well exemplified in the case of applications by lorry owners to carry goods. Apart from those wanting 'C' licences, which entitle them to carry their own goods only, such applicants had to prove that 'suitable transport facilities' were not already available. Any breezy newcomer who asked for a licence simply on the ground that he was willing to risk a little money in the business was wasting his time, for in road transport there was not the slightest chance for him to get started. It was not sufficient for him to prove that a lot of people were willing to give him a trial [1]—this was liable to be regarded as a barefaced attempt to snatch customers away from the old firms, and in any case 'the trader is not the final judge of what form of transport suits his purpose best. That lies with the Licensing Authority and the Tribunal.' [2]

It was not sufficient to state—however odd this may seem for that time—that the reason for the proposed application was to provide employment. Thus the farmer who wanted a lorry licence for his son on the ground that the son would otherwise be unemployed was quite properly sent away with a flea in his ear.[3] And it need hardly be said that it was not sufficient for a new-comer to show that he could run the existing service cheaper.[4] It was not even

[1] Cf. Ponsonby, 'The New Conditions of Entry into the Road Haulage Business', *Economica*, May 1937, p. 202.

[2] Walker, op. cit., p. 144.

[3] Because, as the Chairman of the Tribunal said: 'No evidence was given nor even a suggestion made that the vehicle proposed to be acquired was required to meet the needs of the traders'. Quoted in Ponsonby, op. cit., *Economica*, May 1937.

[4] 'The Tribunal has refused to allow questions of rates as relevant evidence, except in the extreme case where traffic would not pass at all were it not for the lower rate, or where traffic can be shown to be "false", built up by charging rates uneconomical to the applicant.' Walker, op. cit., p. 155.

sufficient to show that the public did in fact patronize a new service which abstracted customers from no one and did not exist before. In Forrester's case, where the applicant had started a goods service connecting Cardiff with the inland villages up the valleys, it was held that the services were so frequent as to be wasteful and unnecessary, and that the natural centres for the villages without direct rail connection with Cardiff were towns other than Cardiff.

Although the old firms in the business of inland transport were thus pretty effectively safeguarded by the licensing system, it does not, of course, follow that they saw eye to eye on all occasions, especially when one of them appeared to be contemplating some extension of service. Thus if a licensed road haulier wanted to expand his business, and applied for a supplementary licence to do so, the railway company might sometimes be found lukewarm about the proposal on the ground that the railway already provided a suitable service. And since the haulier had to prove that his vehicles had been regularly and fully employed during the currency of his last licence and that there had been no material change in the scope of his business, there did not appear to be much encouragement for enterprising hauliers to expand their services, but considerable encouragement for those who wished to stop them from expanding. It is not only the most suspicious-minded critics who find in all these facts a certain implication that the Road and Rail Traffic Act of 1933 was administered ultimately not in the interest of the travelling public and not in the interest of road and rail traffic, but only in the interest of the oldest of the old-established firms—namely, the railway companies.

CHAPTER 6

TRADING LESS

IT is a depressing fact that since the Middle Ages the economic legislation of most sovereign States has reflected two widely held and related beliefs which would certainly have been regarded as uncharitable by the standards of classical antiquity and may perhaps cease to be respectable in our own day when the forces of reason and light prevail. The first of these beliefs is that economic loss when suffered by foreigners is beneath notice; the second is that losses may be thrown on to foreigners without any consequential hardship being borne in the home country.

These beliefs give rise to one of the most dubious though most common forms of restrictionism—namely, that which operates across the national boundary and which seeks in the supposed interests of the home producer to bar foreign products from access to the home market. The contrary view, which has a certain appeal to common sense as well as to humanity in this matter, is that if people want to exchange goods across national boundaries there is no strong prima facie case for preventing them from doing so, since neither party is enforced and both must gain from the transaction, or they would not otherwise engage in it.

But ten years after the last war this view began to lose ground, at first for occult political reasons and esoteric economic ones which the common man did not understand, but later for clear reasons of military preparedness which he did. A certain confusion was created in the public mind when Governments continued to harp dutifully on the once-popular theme of the blessings of free trade immediately after administrative action apparently inspired by the idea that freedom of trade was to be avoided at all costs; [1] and the confusion was not lessened when prominent statesmen urged at Geneva that free trade served the ends of peace, whilst trade barriers were being raised at the same time by all countries in an attempt to safeguard themselves from war. By the late thirties public bewilderment in these matters had reached such an advanced stage that no one was at all surprised when a British Prime Minister, in reply to a peace delegation, argued eloquently that 'the cause of world peace would be promoted by the free exchange of goods and services across the frontiers of nations' [2] a short time after his Government had been responsible for the passage of the Import Duties Act of 1932, which brought to an end nearly a century of British free trade.

TARIFF-MAKING

Nevertheless the presumption in favour of freedom of trade was so firmly fixed in the public mind that tariff-makers, at least in the early years of the inter-war period, felt themselves obliged to go through the intellectual motions of justifying each new obstacle to trade as an unavoidable derogation from what they themselves had thought of (in their undergraduate days) as high economic principle. And from the frequency with which it recurs and the fervour with which it is pressed, the chief special case is clearly that where the foreigner has some advantage in his trade which makes it 'unfair' for his goods to be allowed to compete with the home variety.

This line of argument is of very respectable antiquity. Since Adam Smith pointed out in 1776 that on account of

[1] 'Commercial Policy in the Inter-War Period', League of Nations, Princeton, U.S.A., 1942, Part II, c. 3 and 4.

[2] Speech of the Prime Minister, reported in *The Times*, 25 March 1937.

the weather being rather better in France, Scottish vineyards are greatly handicapped in competition with French vineyards, and Bastiat followed him in the same vein by ascribing the misfortunes of candlemakers to the competition of the sun,[1] there has been a long history of attempts to block imports for the one reason which, at least to the unsophisticated, should make them acceptable—namely, that they are made under more convenient and advantageous conditions abroad. Foreign competition under these conditions is certainly unfair, in the sense that it is unfair between any two persons one of whom does the job much better; but those who want the job well done and will ultimately pay for it—that is, the spending public—can hardly be expected to interest themselves in placing obstacles in the way of the best man doing it. This is why there has been in the past a presumption in favour of free trade in the general interest.

If the canon of 'fairness' in international competition were strictly adhered to, the consequences for the world economy might be rather odd, as all exports, and therefore all imports, would become impossible. This solution was in fact envisaged, with what now looks like uncanny foresight, by the United States in 1922, when the Tariff Act which was passed in that year laid down the rule that whenever home costs were higher than foreign costs, tariffs should be imposed to offset the difference. This way of eliminating international trade altogether in order to make it fair might, it is true, remove a moral blemish from economic life, but it would probably appear to the unfortunate people living under such a régime as one more example of the folly of pouring out the baby with the bath-water.

[1] The Petition of the Tallow Chandlers, Lamp Makers and Others to the House of Commons, cited in the 'Economic Sophisms' of F. Bastiat, adapted by E. R. P. Edgecumbe, London, 1893, p. 42.

When the foreign advantage is low wages, generous hearts as well as muddled heads can be mobilized in the service of restriction. It is this fatal combination which causes spokesmen at international conferences to claim the sympathy of the world not only for the workers of their own country, but for the 'pauper' labour (British if the spokesman is American, Japanese if he is British) employed by their foreign competitors. Experienced observers may perhaps be excused their readiness to detect sometimes a hint of crocodile tears in these proceedings, though the case for higher wages abroad, if necessary by Government action, often looks unanswerable on humanitarian grounds. When the ultimate object is the exclusion of foreign goods, it is immaterial whether the barrier is a tariff at the home port or a high statutory wage level abroad. In either case, if the restriction is effective the foreign worker is worse off than before, though he may prefer the former as the lesser evil. A tariff at least does not shut him out of more than one market, though a higher statutory wage level would.

The very striking differences in wage levels between nations which occur in practice [1] are in large part a consequence of the exclusion of labour wishing to cross national boundaries. But for this exclusion, international wage levels would not differ by more than the proportions customary within the national boundaries of the largest countries at present. Now, it may seem perhaps a little uncharitable to exclude workers from the home labour market by anti-immigration laws and also to exclude by

[1] e.g., in the textile industry:

	Weekly wages per worker (In yen at Dec. 1932 rates)
Japan	5·8
United Kingdom	29·2
United States	84·0

(I.L.O. 'Report on the World Textile Industry', Studies and Reports, B. 27, Vol. 1, p. 208).

tariffs the goods they make. But to urge on humanitarian grounds that their wages should be raised so that their competitive position in the world market is worsened suggests a refinement of hypocrisy. In this matter the Austrian Chamber of Deputies, which in 1924 authorized the Government to increase up to one third the duties on manufactured goods coming from States which had not ratified the Washington Hours Convention, was perhaps unconscious of any inconsistency.[1] Their object—to raise the standards of foreign workers—was entirely laudable; the means—to refuse to buy their products—remain mysterious.

The second special case in which the presumption in favour of free trade is questioned is where there is substantial unemployment in the importing country. Few would deny that tariffs on imports can have the effect in the first instance of maintaining or creating employment, and though many people would say, as Keynes did, that an earthquake would serve the purpose even better, there seem obvious reasons why the more drastic remedy should be treated as a last resort. In practice, however, an increase in employment behind the tariff is apt to mean a decrease outside, and the pre-war experiments made to meet this difficulty are not reassuring. Thus in Roumania before the war it was made illegal to export crude oil in the interests of employment in Roumanian oil refineries. In Hungary, however, there was a duty on refined oil imports. In order to safeguard the stability of employment in both countries therefore, the oil was refined in Roumania, and its parts were then mixed together again and sent into

[1] In 1925 the same idea was voiced in the British House of Commons and in France by the Advisory Committee of Experts to the French Ministry of Commerce. In 1937 the World Textile Conference in Washington suggested that Governments should 'bear in mind standards of international labour conventions in framing their commercial policy'.

Hungary as unrefined oil, where they could be refined once again in the Hungarian refineries.[1] There is a suggestion of waste about this procedure, however, which might perhaps tell against any wide extension of it in the long run.

In the conditions of the early 1920's and of the period following the financial collapse of 1929, a third category of exemptions from the general rule of free trade was held to be justified, where the importing country had a deficit balance of payments. This involved drastic restrictions on imports, because the means of paying for them were short, and a timely expansion of exports to fill the gap seemed unlikely. But such restrictions are the emergency measures for a crisis, not the foundation of a new fiscal gospel—which they seem to have become.

If claims of this sort are to be fairly met, particularly claims of the first and second categories, the tariff level must be carefully adjusted with an eye on the competitive position of the foreign exporter whose goods it is sought to exclude. But it should be said on behalf of the unfortunate tariff-maker that the facts about the level of costs abroad were often exceedingly difficult to obtain. In the pre-war economic world in which rivers ran up hills and the straight road between two points was by no means always the best route, goods were not always priced at cost, and things were not always what they seemed. This was nowhere truer than in the export field. When the interesting discovery was made that more exports are a means of increasing employment without increasing home production, many countries, feeling that the economic problem had at last been solved completely, went in for exports almost in the spirit of a religious revival, with the importing interests (i.e., the bulk of the population in many cases) in the role of insufferable heretics. This is pre-

[1] Haberler, 'Theory of International Trade', London, 1936, p. 347.

sumably why Bulgarian exports just before the war cost less when they were reimported from Germany than when they were bought at home, why German exports over a wide range cost less abroad than at home, and why Australian dairy produce sold at lower prices in England than where it originated 12,000 miles away. Perhaps the Italian exporters who in 1934 offered not only to provide their Austrian customers with flour for nothing, but also to pay the freight on it and to give a bonus of 20 lire per 100 kilogrammes as well,[1] laid themselves open to misconstruction on the subject of what it cost them to produce flour in Italy. But their understanding of economic trends cannot be doubted; and the corresponding bewilderment of the Austrian tariff-makers may be safely assumed.

The problems of the tariff-maker, hampered as he was by ignorance and torn between the sublime innocence of his Prime Minister and the organized rapacity of the trade interests he protected, might have been much simplified if he had found it possible to discriminate between different foreign countries and apply a separate tariff to each. His field of operations was in most cases already covered by a network of commercial treaties and long-period agreements, and numerous rapid changes in tariff rates, applicable to all comers, would have wide and far-reaching repercussions. This consideration, together with the awkward fact of the inconvertibility of many important foreign currencies, made it seem desirable to deal with the trade from each country on separate lines. Before tariffs went out of fashion as an instrument of commercial policy, a final attempt was made to adapt them in different ways to different national groups of exporters in the peculiar conditions of the inter-war period.

[1] The Italians received a large export premium. The object of their manœuvre was to jump a very high Austrian tariff. Pester Lloyd, 25 February 1934, p. 18.

Whatever the advantages of this course to a particular nation, however, it involved in practice the abrogation of 'most favoured treatment', which guaranteed equality of opportunity for the traders of all subscribing nations in the markets of the country conceding it, and which used to be upheld as a norm of international commercial policy by the principal trading nations of the world. The ingenuity of the tariff-makers was now directed to circumventing this rule of equal treatment, and the methods they involved were not without success. A beginning was made when nations insisted on their own customs nomenclature, according to which the addition of a coloured label reading 'This Side Up' might be held to change a cardboard box from 'external packing material' into a 'special luxury article' liable to a heavy duty.[1] Veterinary and health regulations, beginning perhaps with some perfectly innocent arrangement like the British prohibition on the importation of live parrots in 1930 to prevent the spread of psittacosis, but going on to extremes with no scientific justification, were a fertile field for circumventing equality of treatment. The tariff itself might be made very complicated, so that infringements of the equal-treatment rule would be difficult to identify. Thus, in studying the tariff of the Irish Free State before the war, foreign coffin manufacturers must have got a nasty jar when they discovered (if they ever did) that foreign coffins could only be imported into Ireland free of duty if they were brought in by foreigners as a wedding present, the ordinary duty being 50 per cent.[2]

Complicated 'two-' or even 'three-decker' tariffs have long been a popular device for favouring one's economic friends with a low barrier and penalizing enemies with a high one, and as a group constitute a further deliberate

[1] Cf. 'Report of the International Chamber of Commerce', cited in *Manchester Guardian*, 11 July 1938.

[2] Cf. 'The Irish Tariff' in *Economist*, 26 February 1938.

attempt to evade the most-favoured-nation obligation. However, as during the inter-war period not all friends came to be regarded with equal warmth or all enemies to be considered equally insufferable, the number of decks often seemed too few to supply the nice differentiation which the situation required. The German device of defining special categories of the product which could be multiplied at will raised hopes in some quarters at one time that equal treatment in international trade would soon cease to possess any practical significance whatever. The celebrated German preference on milk products coming from 'brown dappled cows reared at a level of at least 300 metres above the sea and passing at least one month in every summer at a height of at least 800 metres',[1] could not be shown to be, on the face of it, a preference to any particular country, though many thoughtful observers took the view that it was in effect a preference in favour of Switzerland against Holland. It is easy to understand, however, that, in spite of these improvements, certain Governments were not entirely converted from old-fashioned views on the subject of equal treatment, while most business men and the wider public came to regard tariff-making as one of the black arts.

QUOTAS

At this point the situation may be said to have been saved by the invention of the quota. The quota is a comparatively new device for restricting imports, though obviously one with a great future. The principle is the complete exclusion of a given class of goods above a given amount. This is clearly a more effective bar than a tariff, which permits unlimited entry on payment of the penalty. But the very strength of this weapon is felt sometimes to be a drawback to its employment. Thus the sudden application of a

[1] Haberler, op. cit., p. 339.

quota will not only raise serious difficulties for exporters, but may sometimes involve embarrassments for the importing country also—especially if the goods cannot be sent back, as in the case of the 27 tons of Turkish eggs sent to France in excess of the quota and destroyed there for reasons which may be surmised.[1] The mere rumour that a quota is impending has often had a most disturbing effect. Thus when the news got about in 1932 that the French Government was contemplating a quota on glue, merchants from all over the world began to pour glue into France, so that the quota was far exceeded in the first quarter. Whatever may be the effects on the foreign exporter, however, from the point of view of the home producer these are minor blemishes.

Official opinion became rapidly wedded to quotas in pre-war years on account of their secrecy and administrative convenience, as in their most advanced forms they could be changed at very short notice without asking anybody's permission, least of all the permission of the legislature. But there has perhaps been a tendency to over-state the case by representing that quotas do not raise internal prices (since the goods enter free of tax), whereas tariffs do. If the quota causes less goods to be imported than would come in without it, however, it is a little difficult to see why the scarcity thus induced should not raise prices, just as a tariff would do—though the foreign exporter pockets the increase this time, not the customs collector.

It is, of course, arguable that the rise in price need not really matter. Some Governments, after all, have attempted to meet whatever drawbacks a high price for imports may be thought to have by instructing one Department to take measures to reduce prices after another Department had just applied a quota and raised them. To judge from the Swiss experience, however, where the Government success-

[1] F. A. Haight, 'French Import Quotas', London, 1935, p. 22.

fully reduced the price to the consumer of tissue-paper and tombstones under these conditions,[1] the victories of the first Department occur on a somewhat narrower front than the victories of the second. Other Governments consider that a high price for imports confers a positive advantage on the importing country, as when a British Minister of Agriculture asserted that if our imports cost us more, this would help the foreigner to buy more of our exports.[2] There is no doubt that on a forward view this would, in time, do much to reduce the foreign dislike for British quotas, because it would permit us to export more and more in exchange for less and less.

The high internal prices brought about by a quota confer monetary advantages on the fortunate importers who can get a share in it, which may account for the popularity of quotas, as against tariffs, amongst them. It may also explain the somewhat obscure and paradoxical means pursued by some Governments to impound these gains for the public. Thus in Switzerland before the war it was necessary to buy home-manufactured zip-fasteners in order to get a licence to import foreign boots under the quota; similarly those who wanted a tombstone from Italy had to buy a Swiss one as well. At first sight this sounds like a scheme for reinforcing the restrictionist effect of the quota—by making it necessary for the importer to charge an even higher price to compensate him for having to buy things he (and the consumer) does not want in addition to things he (and the consumer) does. But this is no doubt an over-simplified and prejudiced interpretation of a very complex state of affairs.

As further experience was accumulated in what may perhaps be called the Indian summer of the quota régime from 1937 onwards, the trade associations of importers

[1] H. Heuser, 'Control of International Trade', London, 1939, p. 239. [2] Pigou, 'Economics in Practice', London, 1935, p. 15.

were called in and more systematic arrangements were made for distributing the quota amongst them. These bodies may usually be relied on to distribute allocations to those who have been longest in the trade, though it is perhaps not always clear that length of service in the trade is a reliable indicator of efficiency. At any rate, the Swiss practice of basing the shares on the 1913 imports seems almost to have elevated this doctrine into a form of ancestor worship, agreeable enough, no doubt, to elderly business men like the fruit importer who sold his share to a competitor for four thousand francs a year and retired on the proceeds, but perhaps not conceived in the best interests of efficiency.

The competition of business men in the importing country for a share in the quota is likely to be paralleled by competition amongst exporters for what may be an equally profitable share of the business on their side. Sooner or later the advantage of a united front to exclude outsiders and maximize the individual firm's share of the spoil is likely to occur to a few enlightened persons in both groups, who will seek to simplify the complexities of competition on a thousand fronts into a single deal between a monopolistic trade association of importers and a monopolistic trade association of exporters. Where such bodies already exist, Governments wishing to impose quotas have an easy task. Any slight hesitation the traders may feel about accepting a quota régime may be overcome if the Government concerned deliberately fixes the amount so that at the resulting market price both parties share in the gains—i.e., the importers get more for importing less and the exporters get more for selling less. A condition of success is, of course, that new-comers to the business, attracted by the high level of earnings in it, must be rigorously excluded. And a likely consequence of the whole procedure is that the prices at which the goods are finally exchanged will bear only a remote relation to the costs of producing them, and will depend ultimately on how far each group of producers can go in persuading the one Government to bring pressure to bear on the other.

EXCHANGE CONTROL

At all times of economic disturbance the Government is inevitably cast for the role of *deus ex machina* ready to rush from the wings in the last act in order to restore order after a rather indiscriminate slaughter of the apparently wicked and rehabilitation of the apparently virtuous. In the comedy of errors in commercial policy during the inter-war period, quotas may be said to have advanced the entry by one act; exchange control to have advanced it by two. Although exchange control may begin as an unofficial exercise of their discretion by commercial banks, it is fatally liable in practice, to judge from pre-war experience, to involve intervention by the Government at a very early stage, and on a scale which rapidly brings all foreign trade transactions under Government control.

Exchange control in the sense used here means much more than the periodical appearance on the exchange market of a Government Stabilization Fund as a large buyer or seller amongst other buyers and sellers. This somewhat timid method of intervention is available only to rather rich Governments who can afford to accumulate big Funds. Moreover, it obliges Governments to take the awkward decision about what general rate the Fund should aim at producing in the market. Although advice from exporters can always be obtained suggesting that the rate is far too high,[1] and from importers (though not so easily) suggesting

[1] British exporters (and others) regarded the British Exchange Fund as a device for keeping the pound weak. Cf. letter of the Parliamentary Monetary Committee in *The Times*, 25 November 1938: 'We suggest that the authorities in charge of the Exchange Equalization Fund shall revert to its original intention and place their ability and resources at the disposal of British exporters. . . .'

that the rate is far too low, Governments often found it difficult to come to a decision before the war, and cast unhappily around for some better method of controlling the exchanges which would please both exporters and importers by abolishing the market altogether and if necessary applying a different rate of exchange to each product. This is essentially what 'Exchange Control' means.

As soon as a Control in this sense is set up, it immediately cuts across tariffs, quotas, and other old-fashioned restrictions. However much at home he may feel with the forbidding technicalities of the exchanges,[1] and however skilled he may be at piloting his goods through the Customs Houses, it may be safely said that no exporter will go on exporting if he does not receive any payment whatever for his goods. Import licences from the Ministry of Commerce are not very helpful if the National Bank will only allot 20 per cent of the foreign exchange required to pay the bill or will allot 30 per cent on condition that the goods are bought from some other country, or will allot 40 per cent on condition that unwanted bath-tubs are bought from Ireland as well as wanted silk stockings from Czechoslovakia. On the other hand, if Ruritanian currency *is* on offer at the National Bank, and silk stockings may be bought with it, importers are likely to accept them from this source, whatever their quality, rather than wait for the chance of getting a payment through to their usual suppliers if the latters' currency happens to be short. Exchange

[1] In the House of Commons on 21 December 1920, Lt.-Col. Hurst is reported to have said: 'Of course this subject of foreign exchanges is one I know very little about and I believe very few people do know anything about it. Indeed, I have read that only one person knows the real arcana of the foreign exchanges and he is in a lunatic asylum. The late Lord Goschen was thought to know something about it. . . .' (Cited by T. E. Gregory in 'Foreign Exchanges', Oxford, 1935.)

controls can thus be used to strengthen commercial policy.

There is a happy illustration of this from pre-war British policy. The prevailing economic doctrine at that time was to 'buy from those that buy from us'. This simple rule, which would have put nearly everybody out of work and turned the entire British people into a race of pastoral nomads if it had been applied *inside* the national boundary, was popularly supposed, for some mysterious reason, to be completely beneficial when applied to foreign trade; and the British Government had in fact considerable success in recommending small nations to buy more British goods if they did not wish to see their own exports excluded from the British market. Thus in 1933, in a provisional trade agreement with Estonia 'the Estonian Government recognizes that it is in the interest of both countries that the present disparity in that balance (of trade) should be re-adjusted as far as possible by the increase of the sale in Estonia of goods the produce or manufacture of the United Kingdom'.[1] In such agreements it was fully intended that the balancing of trade should be effected by the use of exchange controls, which had to be set up by the smaller countries if they did not exist already.

Exchange controls and trade policy being so clearly complementary, it is usually not long before a convenient marriage is arranged between the National Bank and the Ministry of Commerce. Payments and permits for all goods and services passing across national frontiers now become centralized in one institution, and harassed bureaucrats now empowered to apply a special, arbitrary, and if necessary secret rate of exchange (alterable at will) to any group of transactions (defined at will), regret the years they spent coaxing tariffs through a reluctant legislature

[1] Cited in 'Trade Relations between Free-Market and Controlled Economies', League of Nations, Geneva, 1943.

and wonder why they did not think of it before. It is perhaps ungracious to reflect, after contemplation of the frequent kaleidoscopic changes in the rates, regulations, definitions, and conditions of the pre-war controlled exchange market, that exchange controls were originally introduced because variations in rates under free conditions were held to be so uncertain and unpredictable.

Once the Control has got into its stride, its possibilities of public service are extensive and peculiar. Many elegant tricks of commercial diplomacy would be impossible without it. The Germans, for example, invented a very refined way of repudiating their foreign debts. The German Government, whose citizens had borrowed large sums abroad by the flotation of securities on foreign money markets, prevented its citizens from paying interest on those securities by rationing the currency needed for this purpose. The foreign creditors naturally found the value of their securities fell heavily, whereupon the agents of the German exchange control relieved them from all further embarrassments by buying their holdings for next to nothing and repatriating them. Another popular way of getting something for nothing out of the foreigner by means of exchange control is to fix exchange rates so that the national currency is ' over-valued '—i.e., is sold at more than it is really worth in terms of purchasing power over the home products. This causes importers to buy too much because foreign goods are made artificially cheap in the home currency, and exporters to sell too little because home goods are made artificially dear in the foreign currency. As imports will exceed exports under these conditions, debt accumulates, generally to the great surprise of the creditor. Various ways may now be diffidently suggested by the debtor of settling this debt on terms which the creditor would never have accepted if he had seen through the trick in the first place.

Whatever the appeal of economic prestidigitation of this

kind to needy or disreputable Governments, it is not always popular amongst the citizens. Under the free system individual exporters are accustomed to sell the proceeds of their exports for foreign money, which is then transferred by the banks to importers, who spend it on buying things that they think people at home will want. Under the system of exchange control the introduction of the device of the 'blocked balance' precludes the banks from making such transfers except under particular conditions laid down by Government—for example, as to the rate of exchange or as to the kinds of goods which may be purchased. It is true that this procedure often 'facilitates' international trade by making possible particular deals which would not take place without it, but on the definition of trade as an operation by which people are enabled to exchange things they do not want for things they do want, results are sometimes a little puzzling. Thus a certain dismay must have been felt by Americans with no ear for music but large blocked mark balances in Germany, when they learnt in June 1936 that the Standard Oil Company of New Jersey had taken over forty million mouth organs from Germany in payment for blocked marks held there.[1] Roumanians in a similar position must have felt equally anxious when they heard a little later that Roumania was 'submerged under a flood of accordions' for similar reasons.[2]

It is perhaps not surprising that in face of these somewhat unexpected methods of repaying debts, creditors should have sought at an early stage to evade the Control, as for example by buying jewels in Germany with their blocked marks and smuggling the jewels over the frontier for sale abroad; or buying mortgaged property and paying off the mortgage (all in blocked marks) and borrowing

[1] *The Times*, 3 June 1936, cited in League of Nations 'World Economic Survey 1935–6', p. 198.

[2] A. Piatier, 'L'Economie de Guerre', Paris, 1939, p. 194.

again on mortgage in free marks which could then be sold outside the Control.[1] The calendar of crimes in this connexion was a steadily lengthening one before the war, and many were the village Hampdens whose doubtless misguided ingenuity added considerably to it; as, for example, the eight farmers on the Dutch–German frontier who fed their hens on cheap grain in Holland and taught them to lay their eggs on the German side of the frontier, thus smuggling two million eggs across at a handsome profit and without paying duty.[2] These malefactors received five months imprisonment for contravention of the exchange control regulations.

Such a penalty might perhaps have been viewed by an uncharitable critic as a confession on the part of the controllers, however numerous, expert, and well-paid, that they were no match for the wits of the controlled, who are always regrettably more numerous, though sometimes poor and ignorant. In Germany the controllers seem to have adopted this view with characteristic thoroughness, for at a comparatively early stage they took the next logical step of imposing the death penalty for 'egotistical' transfers of capital abroad in contravention of the foreign exchange regulations.[3] Though it is likely that the essential principle of what may be called decapitatory exchange control would, if widely extended, ultimately make any economic system work, since only those in agreement with it would be left alive, its use in this case may well be thought a little precipitous, and rather an unfortunate climax to the well-intentioned efforts of Governments to intervene helpfully in international trade.

[1] A. Piatier, 'Le Contrôle de Devises', Paris, 1937, p. 115.

[2] *News Chronicle*, 16 December 1935, cited in League of Nations 'World Economic Survey 1935–6', p. 196.

[3] The German decree of 1 December 1936 imposing the death penalty is quoted in Piatier, 'Le Contrôle de Devises', p. 120.

CHAPTER 7

THE POLITICS OF RESTRICTIONISM

AS a subject for economic melodrama, 'pressure groups' held the stage for many years after the first World War, and even to-day it is possible that some people could be got to believe that all wars are caused by 'the international armament ring', or that the decline in morals is due to lobbying in the House of Lords by the lipstick trust. The facts are that since most acts of State have economic repercussions, it has always been customary for the persons affected thereby to form groups and associations in order to try to influence the political process whenever it seemed to their advantage to do so. Under the democratic system, where power—to the despair of many reformers—still inevitably resides in numbers, this is hardly a surprising development. Any form of democratic politics expects, indeed almost requires, that citizens holding strong views on any matters which are the concern of government should make their views known to the Government and to as many of their fellow-citizens as possible in any lawful way which seems appropriate to them. In this country a League of British Busybodies may be formed (and doubtless has been formed) to espouse any legal cause whatsoever.

In the economic sphere a convenient engine of propaganda on behalf of group interests frequently lies ready to hand in the professional associations, trade unions, and trade associations which may have been formed originally to do the spadework of settling family quarrels in particular industries. In recent years, and especially in the inter-war period, a peculiar change has occurred in the activities of these bodies, which have not only enlarged their propaganda activities but have come much closer to the Government itself, and in many cases have turned into appendages of the Government machinery. No doubt the tiresome business of collective bargaining over wage rates and conditions of work, which was their primary function, must often have seemed an exhausting struggle, in which the honours were few and seldom very evenly divided between the parties, and the returns in the long run incommensurate with the cost. Nevertheless the enthusiasm with which economic groups have thrown themselves into the more profitable and less arduous task of cultivating the political field is undoubtedly a remarkable phenomenon of modern times.

Some of the earliest instances of this phenomenon amongst workers' organizations occurred after the passage of the Trade Union Act of 1913, which empowered Trade Unions to use their funds for political action. Although no doubt had arisen about the freedom of employers' organizations to contribute to what, in their view, were deserving political causes, the interest of business men as a whole in the machinery of government did not become very close until the first World War, a time when contacts between Government and business were numerous and extensive, and when it was felt to be a great convenience if Government and ' the industry ' could speak to one another through the mouths of a few men seated round a table. In 1918 the Balfour Committee [1] thought it ' very desirable that in all important British industries there should exist strong, comprehensive and well-organized associations ', and advised the Government to encourage them. As has been shown in previous chapters, there is no doubt about the seriousness with which the Government took this advice. As a result, old associations took on a new lease

[1] ' Final Report of the Committee on Commercial and Industrial Policy after the War ', Cd. 9035, 1918, p. 35.

of life and new ones sprang up to adorn the industrial scene in all sorts of unexpected places. Nearly twenty years later, speaking of what might almost be called the period of hot-house growth, the Prime Minister explained that 'there was a great growth of voluntary organization in industry because it was recognized that as contacts with Government became closer, it was convenient and almost necessary, to set up in each industry some central organizing or governing body which could, on behalf of the industry, watch what the Government was doing'.[1] The language is perhaps not very happy, but the point of view is unmistakable. And no doubt there *are* advantages for Government officials in being able to 'consult the industry' or to 'ascertain the views of the workers' by telephoning to the Secretary of a Trade Association or Trade Union at an office within easy walking distance of Westminster. It remains to ask at what cost they are secured.

THE INFLUENCE OF ECONOMIC GROUPS

The ways in which organized economic groups can exercise political pressure are numerous, obscure, and occasionally mysterious, depending much on the personal qualities of the group officials and very much on the political machinery and the political atmosphere at particular times. The importance of the officials can be underestimated. The office of President or *a fortiori* of Secretary of a Trade Association or Trade Union calls for high qualities of tact, resourcefulness, and experience in public relations, and nowadays it is quite customary for these uncommon qualities to be placed more and more frequently at the disposal of powerful Trade Associations in consideration of emoluments which in some cases can only be described as dazzling. High officials of Trade Associations

[1] *The Times*, 15 October 1937.

may or may not be persons of considerable experience in the industry themselves. Their primary duties do not demand it. These duties are to inform the public of the dignity and importance of the industry and of the value of its product, to remove misconceptions about its activities in the Press, and generally to paint a picture for the public eye of a well-deserving if rather ill-rewarded group of people, joined together in a mysterious entity called ' the industry ', and all distinguished by a single-minded devotion to the service of a somewhat stony-hearted public which has been too long ignorant of the burdens of its uncomplaining servants.

In this way a certain amount of political support from the general public for a particular industry can no doubt be generated. But the most profitable point of attack nowadays, where the personal qualities of the Trade Association Secretary count most heavily, is the Government machine itself. Thus at all important official inquiries the economic interests which consider themselves affected offer, and in many cases are asked for, evidence through the medium of their representative groups; the list of such witnesses sometimes makes interesting reading.[1] Groups interested in securing a tariff on imports now make their case direct to the Import Duties Advisory Committee, which encouraged the formation of Trade Associations for the purpose. Group representatives find their way on to several administrative bodies semi-officially connected with various Government Departments, officials of the groups are constantly memorializing Ministers and calling on Government officials, and periodically, eminent deputations

[1] The Committee recently reporting to the Minister of Labour on the Rehabilitation of the Catering Industry consulted nearly thirty Trade Associations, ranging from the Brewers Society to the Eel Pie Traders Association and the Coffee-Stall Keepers Protection Association.

from the most important groups sally forth to try conclusions with the Chancellor of the Exchequer.

In time of war or near-war the services of these bodies become indispensable. In the last few years they have been consulted on such vital matters as labour direction, materials allocation, price control, and zoning. Their staffs are sometimes taken over *en bloc* by the Government,[1] their senior officials become Controllers and their Presidents become Ministers; alternatively, they are attached to Government Departments in an advisory capacity, often with direct access to the Minister and in continuous contact with his officials. In the export field, for instance, the British trade associations recently formed, or helped to form, nearly three hundred Export Groups, which received bulk supplies of controlled materials for distribution to their members engaged in the export trade, and sometimes to members in the home trade too. Export Groups and Trade Associations also co-operated with the Board of Trade in the war-time concentration of production on particular types of goods and in particular firms, and in the allocation of coupons for the manufacture of products made out of rationed materials. This is the situation in one section of a large Department. But the process of administrative incrustation has spread in practice to all the principal Departments. The Ministry of Food, in particular, *created* about fifty combines and associations of traders, and entrusted much of its detailed administrative work to them. It seems highly improbable that very many layers of the crust will be scraped off within measurable distance of the end of the war.[2]

Economic groups normally focus their main political

[1] e.g., the Iron and Steel Control was merely the Iron and Steel Federation under another name.

[2] Cf. 'The Relations of Trade Associations with Government', *Planning*, October 1945.

pressure on Ministers of the Government. These hapless creatures may be waited upon, memorialized, written to, telephoned, dined, or got at through their friends in the interest of some particular industry. If the pressure is strong enough they may have to answer questions in Parliament artfully framed by a member of the group, receive deputations led by their political opponents, address meetings chiefly attended by their enemies smarting under some recent legislation, and consider monstrous and fantastic proposals which call for righteous indignation and strong language rather than the serious attention which is invariably promised and occasionally given. In normal times a good Minister who is a target for this kind of importunity can protect himself by playing off one group against another. But once the Government begins to dispense economic favours to particular industries, this procedure leads only to embarrassment, of which the inter-war period furnishes many uncomfortable examples. This is the point at which troubles begin. The mere existence of pressure groups is a normal incident of political life; it is when they begin to compete for favours that they become obnoxious. The power of determined, numerous, and well-organized sectional interests, such as farmers and retail shop-keepers, to 'swing votes' if their share of the spoil is denied them is well known to experienced politicians. Interventionist Governments need Ministers of quite exceptional strength if their policy is not to degenerate into a more or less open levy on the public for the benefit of those particular sectional interests which happen to be most adept at making the lives of politicians a burden to them.

On the assumption, so often justified by events, that the Minister bows to the inevitable, his official advisers in the Department are nearly powerless to intervene, whatever their own views may be of the requirements of the public interest. This does not imply agreement with the view expressed by many politicians who have never held office, that civil servants are the lowest form of life in the political world. On the contrary, these 'men of oil, steel, and silk', in the words of W. L. George, are not at all the characterless cyphers which the principle of constitutional anonymity and their administrative subordination to Ministers would imply. It stands to reason, given the great extension of Government activities in the economic field, that no Minister temporarily in charge of a large Department of anything up to five or six thousand officials can have anything but a very hazy idea of all the work that goes on in it, and that in the nature of the case more and more discretionary power has had to be given to the officials themselves. The point is certainly not lost on the latter, who, where their views conflict with those of the Minister, are normally accustomed to refer contentious matters to him before taking action. If, under present-day conditions, the Minister is a bad one or is unduly sensitive to the pressure of some economic interest, the loyal civil servant who is at the same time a firm believer in Parliamentary democracy, as most of them are, is brought sharply up against the old dilemma—that a bad Minister may be obeyed to the letter by his subordinates, which is bad government but good democracy; or he may be disobeyed in stealth by his subordinates, which may be good government but is certainly bad democracy. Of course the lines of this dilemma are seldom so sharply drawn in practice; but the fact that it is inescapable under interventionist governments must have struck many public-spirited officials with peculiar force at certain times in the last twenty years. The signs of indignant revolt are not yet very obvious; but to the careful observer they are certainly there. It is possible that the optimistic view expressed by Dale [1] that

[1] 'The Higher Civil Service', Oxford, 1941, p. 139.

'bureaux have grown, but not bureaucracy' may not survive a period of interventionist governments tied too closely to the sectional interests which are behind them.

DELEGATED LEGISLATION

The cause at work is not only the increasing size of Government Departments; the fact is that Parliamentary democracy is in full retreat on several much more important fronts. The central conception of democracy in this country, that Parliament is the sole law-making body and that the civil service exists merely to execute those laws, is becoming lost to sight amidst the thorny political problems raised by large-scale State interventions in the economic field. In early times, and in the then virginal condition of the Statute Book, Parliament could and did pass laws concerning the doing of particular things to particular persons, as when it ordained that the Bishop of Rochester's cook should be boiled to death 'without having any advantage of his clergy'.[1] But the time for legislation in such detail is now long past; and the claim that laws to meet the alleged needs of the period 1919–39 could be framed on any but the broadest lines can be easily refuted by reference to the facts of that period in Chapters 2–6. It is these facts which explain the practice which has grown up in all democratic countries of delegating legislative power to Ministers. In this country the delegation may take the form of the helpful clause: 'For executing the powers given to him by this Act, the Minister shall make such rules and orders as he may think fit . . .'; or, under the terms of the so-called Henry VIII clause, the Minister may be given power to 'modify the provisions of the Act so far as may appear to him to be necessary for the purpose of bringing the Act into operation'.

Under these and similar delegated powers, Statutory

[1] 22 Hen. 8, c. 9.

Orders and Departmental Regulations may be issued which become part of the law of the land, and which may convey powers of economic life and death over whole industries. Thus the Board of Trade had power, under the Safeguarding of Industries Act of 1921, to impose 33⅓ per cent *ad valorem* duties on imported goods at its discretion, and the Treasury, acting on a recommendation of the Import Duties Advisory Committee, was subsequently given similar powers.

The exercise of these powers, in important cases under the eye of the Minister himself, but in other cases at the discretion of his officials, can of course be challenged through the appropriate constitutional channels, particularly if the interests specially affected are organized in an Association with its headquarters near the seat of government. But the sole democratic safeguard of the *public* interest is in the period during which the Orders must be 'laid before the House' of Commons; and since it is obvious that the average Member has neither the time nor the expert knowledge [1] to investigate the hundreds of Orders which pour forth annually from the Departments on every conceivable subject, this safeguard can hardly be taken very seriously. And in fact periodical waves of Parliamentary misgiving on the subject [2] testify to the scepticism with which it is regarded in the House of Commons itself.

What might be called the logic of State interventionism has obliged Parliament to give Government Departments

[1] Non-experts may appropriately study the melancholy paragraphs on 'Quasi-Sub-Legislation' in C. K. Allen's 'Law and Orders', London, 1945.

[2] The latest revival of the controversy produced a debate in the House of Commons on 26 May 1943, in which the Government accepted a motion that 'Parliament should vigilantly maintain its ancient right and duty of examining legislation whether delegated or otherwise'. A Select Committee was appointed in June 1944 to scrutinize Statutory Rules and Orders.

not only legislative powers, but quasi-judicial powers as well, as where a Department or Government bureau has statutory permission, after ascertaining the facts of a case, to use its discretion in administering the appropriate legislation. Thus the Traffic Commissioners under the Road Traffic Act of 1930 have discretion in awarding licences to private transport undertakings, and the Minister of Transport, under the same Act, can hear appeals from their decision. Similarly the Ministry of Labour has power to disallow claims to unemployment benefit under the Unemployment Insurance Acts. It may well be said that these are not matters on which the judgement of a court of law is likely to be useful; but perverse democrats are perhaps entitled in reply to point out the dangers of jumping out of the frying-pan into the fire by making Government officials judges in their own cause and independent (unlike every other citizen) of the impartial judiciary.

GOVERNMENT BY COMMISSION

In the continuous flight from Parliamentary democracy under the pressure of increasing economic interventionism, a final artifice of harassed Governments is exemplified by the delegation of powers not by Parliament to a Ministry, but by a Ministry to a permanent Board or Commission which is not subject to day-to-day criticism in the legislative chamber itself. This practice has developed rapidly in recent times, when bodies like the Road Board, the Forestry Commission and the National Health Insurance Commissioners were set up to relieve the appropriate Minister from continuous questioning in Parliament, and to provide impartial judgement and continuity of policy in matters which were rather lightly assumed to be exempt from violent political controversy. There is a certain melancholy interest in the historical fact that the Haldane Committee of 1918 regarded the spread of these bodies into the economic field with great suspicion.[1] But, given the economic philosophy of the inter-war period, it was quite inevitable; and many such bodies were in fact then established with very far-reaching economic powers. Realistic students of the subject are apt to say that their main purpose in practice was to protect the Minister from political pressure in the dispensation of public favours, though their functions varied from those of the Public Assistance Board, which paid in cash, to those of the Statutory Commissioners set up under the Livestock Subsidy Act of 1937 and the Sea Fish Industry Act of 1938, where the favours took other forms. If the political pressure is strong, however, it seems curious that it should have been purged of all evil by these expedients, and not merely diverted to where its effects were not so obvious. The tyro in these matters may at any rate draw the conclusion that decisions on political questions under these novel conditions are either shaped according to the policy of the Minister ultimately responsible, when the need for the Board is not obvious, or according to the will of the

[1] 'It has been said that there are certain functions of Government which require for their exercise a judicial temper and a position of independence that cannot be maintained by a Minister who is constantly exposed to criticism in Parliament. It was no doubt for these reasons that a special form of constitution was developed in the case of the Road Board and the Development Commission; and we have observed a tendency to recommend the adoption of a similar procedure in the case of various bodies which it is proposed to set up in order to further the economic development of the country after the war.

'We are so far from thinking that the importance of a service to the community is prima facie a reason for making those who administer it immune from ordinary Parliamentary criticism that we feel that all such proposals should be most carefully scrutinized, and that there should be no omission, in the case of any particular service, of those safeguards which Ministerial responsibility to Parliament alone provides.' Report of the Committee on the Machinery of Government, 1918, Cd. 9230, p. 11.

Board, which is a little difficult to distinguish from bureaucracy, however near to archangels the bureaucrats may be.

Individually, these derogations from Parliamentary sovereignty may seem of slight importance. Collectively, they leave an impression of the gradual and ultimately dangerous weakening of democratic control. In pre-war times the charitably minded might say that the process had produced no worse effects than the embarrassment of a few civil servants, who in the exercise of authority properly delegated to them by Parliament had to take over the office of law-maker, when they were practically independent of the legislature, and of judge, when they were completely independent of the judiciary.[1] The reassurances of the Donoughmore Committee on Ministers' Powers [2] that these embarrassments were not serious in the early thirties were no doubt accepted with relief by such. To others the fact that public servants do not operate in a political vacuum must have become increasingly obvious in the succeeding years. Some of the less credulous may perhaps have thought it unwise, and most may have thought it unfair, that public servants endowed with extraordinary powers, and responsible only in more and more remote ways to Parliament, should be exposed to pressures they are constitutionally ill-equipped to resist.

[1] The ordinary Courts can of course decide whether the actions of a Minister or his officials are within the ostensible scope of their authority. But they cannot consider whether discretionary powers have been wisely used or not, and it would be clearly improper to ask them to.

[2] Cd. 4060, 1932, para. 14. 'Power under the Henry VIII clause has been used with the best possible motives. . . . We dispose in passing of the suggestion, unsupported as it is by the smallest shred of evidence, that the existence of such provisions in certain Acts of Parliament is due directly or indirectly to any attempt or desire on the part of members of the permanent Civil Service to secure for themselves or for their Departments an arbitrary power.'

ECONOMIC GROUPS AND POST-WAR PROBLEMS

Whether the peculiar changes which have come over Parliamentary democracy in recent years justify all these suspicions or not, the temptation must be resisted to make a scapegoat of the pressure groups themselves, and thus to miss the real villain of the piece. It is a little difficult to understand why anyone past the undergraduate stage should expect any group of ordinary men called together for the special purpose of representing some sectional economic interest to recommend any course of action for Government but that which is in the interest of their constituents. And presumably nobody outside of Bedlam would expect to discover what is demanded for the public good by taking advice from economic groups whose interest is first to preserve their members, efficient or inefficient, and then to supply the public with worse, dearer, or fewer goods than would be produced if the groups did not exist.

It is an attractive idea to set aside any trifling doubts for the moment and to imagine *all* the interests represented round the table simultaneously. This, to be sure, would greatly relieve the pressure on harassed Ministers and their official servants; but those who expect ultimate wisdom to emerge out of a compromise between the interests would be disappointed. For the interest of the consumer cannot, in the nature of things, be represented at all. The consumer, who is nowadays thought of as a sort of dim and legendary bogey man of old and forgotten economic text-books, is still in practice not quite without importance. In one aspect he is everybody, and it is precisely in that aspect that he is inarticulate. And this is quite inevitable, for although people can be induced to form economic groups in order to better their money incomes, they would normally find it unprofitable to belong to a separate group for every one of the hundreds of things they spend their incomes on.

The present time is an unusual opportunity of resolving any doubts or hesitations on these points which may be felt by the sceptical. Several of the specialized industrial groups and their parent bodies have begun to commit themselves to views on economic reconstruction after the war, and it is not without interest to picture the post-war world as it would be if the trade groups had their way. Not unnaturally, most groups look forward to a more prosperous and more important position for themselves; though in at least one case, where the Chairman of the National Federation of Fish Friers recently[1] committed his Federation to the essentially modest post-war aim that 'people must be able to walk into fish-frying shops and maintain their dignity', the customer came first. On the whole, however, those who turn to such pronouncements expecting to find daring new thoughts and economic inspiration will be disappointed; they will find only proposals which recall with many a nostalgic phrase the pre-war régime, and particularly the already well-known principle of economic Peace and Quiet with the minimum of Government 'interference' and the maximum of Government protection from all the economic winds that blow. To the good reasons which already existed for this attitude may be added the paralysing fears which beset most business men when they contemplate the extreme riskiness of all forms of economic activity in the confusion and kaleidoscopic changes of the post-war world.

The implications of Peace and Quiet are stability of earnings, stability of prices, security of markets, and similar elusive goals so avidly pursued before 1939. The reformers are consequently against competition, 'which leads often to uneconomic investment and production and the final closing down of businesses through unprofitable trad-

[1] *The Times*, 1 June 1943.

ing';[1] they are against outsiders speculating in the staple markets,[2] and they oppose freedom of trade with its associations of instability and uncertainty from the pre-war period. 'Industry has a lively recollection of the effects of unrestricted and often uneconomic competition in the home market by overseas industries before a reasonable measure of protection was granted to home producers.'[3]

On the other hand, they produce ever more ingenious proposals for (Government) guarantees of prices, particularly in agriculture, (Government) guarantees of profits, and the elimination of price fluctuations (by Government action). The farmers' groups, including the Royal Agricultural Society, the National Farmers Union, and the Central Landowners Association, have pressed strongly for the stabilization of 'reasonable' price levels, and the first-named body proposed to link guaranteed wages to guaranteed prices.[4] Some industrialists, not altogether oblivious of the way the wind is blowing, ask why, if food and raw material prices are to be stabilized by Government action, should not manufactured goods be treated in the same way? 'Before the war, production and marketing agreements were in force affecting various kinds of primary products.... It is worthy of consideration whether this policy should be extended to cover manufactured goods, and it might well

[1] 'A National Policy for Industry', Statement of 120 business men, November 1942.

[2] e.g.: In order to eliminate illegitimate speculation, the Association of British Chambers of Commerce recommends that 'dealings in foodstuffs and raw materials should be restricted to those individuals and firms who are directly concerned in the production, manufacture or distribution of the products'. 'Report of the Special Committee on Post-War Industrial Reconstruction of the Association of British Chambers of Commerce', 1942.

[3] 'Report on "Reconstruction" by the Federation of British Industries', 1942.

[4] 'Report of the Committee on Post-war Agricultural Policy of the Royal Agricultural Society.'

prove to be the solution to the problem of controlled ebb and flow of world trade.' Thus the Association of British Chambers of Commerce and, identical in substance, the World Trade Alliance of Sir Edgar Jones.[1] Elaborating on this theme, many business men engaged in foreign trade feel that the uncertainties of their position could be relieved if markets were divided by agreement and fixed quantities at given prices allocated to particular suppliers. As the author of one of these schemes characteristically says, 'We shall have to rebuild security by managed trade before we can take further risks'.[2]

Although in most of these schemes the Government is expected either to give a guarantee of stability to the industry itself or to stand behind it in some way, there is considerable agreement amongst the groups in their opposition to 'bureaucratic interference'. 'Any suggestion for a more permanent system of association of Government with industry should be fully discussed with industry,' says the Federation of British Industries, 'and . . . carried out by agreement and in collaboration with industry itself. The danger of bureaucratic influence . . . must be avoided.'[3] 'Bureaucracy', says the Wholesale Textile Association, 'feeds and fosters the black market.'[4] The General Council of British Shipping finds it 'awful to contemplate a situation when a normal incident of commercial competition will become an Act of State'.[5] Industrialists 'have had such a disheartening experience of the dead hand of White-

[1] 'World Trade Alliance—A Practical Solution of the Problem of Unemployment after the War', London, 1943.

[2] Letter of Sir R. Streat, Chairman of the Cotton Control Board, to *The Times*, 21 July 1941.

[3] 'Report of the Federation of British Industries', already quoted.

[4] 'Report of the Post-war Reconstruction Committee of the Wholesale Textile Association', 1943.

[5] 'Freedom and Efficiency—A Policy for Britain's Merchant Fleet', General Council of British Shipping, 1943.

hall during the past two years', writes Mr. Samuel Courtauld.[1] They fear that 'the Government link would give greater opportunities for graft—not by Government servants but because Government servants are apt to be so easily hoodwinked by crooks. Apart from financial corruption, industrialists would bitterly resent business decisions being influenced by party motives of any kind.'

As the majority of business men who have thought about their post-war prospects at all seem to agree that Government control in some form is inevitable, the problem is to discover a form which cannot be described as 'bureaucratic'. Those unused to quiet reflection and polite language are apt to insist more or less violently that at all costs Civil Servants must be kept out of it; the more learned groups call for 'a new technique of public administration', including the recruitment of 'new types' of men and women. It would be a naïve misconception of these proposals to suggest that their main point is that there should be more public officials and that they should all get higher salaries. Their argument, in less crude language, is that at every strategic point in the economic system there should be stationed a kind of economic archangel in the pay of the State, who, when it comes to the determination of prices, wages, output, and distributors' margins, will supervise without interfering, arbitrate like Solomon between the interests, and generally purge the economic world of its wickedness.

Angels of this rarer kind are to be appropriately accommodated in Government Departments, but plenty of niches for the grosser sort can be found on the Boards of Public Corporations, which many reformers wish to see set up for each key industry. These Corporations are to be chartered by the Government with a monopoly of all business,

1 'Future Relations of Government and Industry', *Economic Journal*, April 1942.

provided with a Government-appointed Board, and operated within narrow legal limits of price, profits, quality of output, &c., like a public utility company, with complete freedom from direct Government interference with day-to-day administration. The fascination which this sort of economic escapism exercises over those whose minds fly readily to remedies of last resort is quite remarkable, and a long line of distinguished advocates of Public Corporations in industries, varying from transport (including railways, roads, canals, coast-wise shipping, and internal air lines)[1] to banks [2] and bacon manufacture,[3] attests the complete conviction of a wider public.

For those who cannot swallow the idea of a Public Corporation for each industry, the humble Trade Association may be offered as an appropriate focal point for Government control. Thus in all the best statements of the new doctrines Trade Associations are given a place of special importance and Government officials get a place of honour in the Association hierarchy. 'Every encouragement should be given to the development of Trade Associations', say the Chambers of Commerce, in a statement typical of many issued by trading bodies on this subject. 'Every effort should be made to maintain and expand them and to bring to their membership all new entrants to individual industries.' Equal enthusiasm is shown by exporters for Export Groups and by agricultural reformers for Marketing Boards. The most varied provisions are made for the link with Government, but it is usually felt that the Association ought to be the interpreter, if not the executive organ of official policy. The Govern-

[1] Speech of Lord Reith in House of Lords, 17 June 1942.

[2] 'Christianity and the Social Order', by the Archbishop of Canterbury, London, 1942, p. 87.

[3] 'A Post-war Agricultural Policy for Great Britain', Memorandum prepared by a Group of Peers, February 1943, p. 15.

ment should delegate to it 'the task of carrying out the national and international policy' in shipping; it should 'act in conjunction with the Board of Trade' in textiles. One elaborate proposal contemplates the supervision of the Trade Associations in the major industries by more refined versions of the same thing, consisting of Public Industrial Boards representing industry, labour, and marketing, and led by a State-appointed Chairman.[1] But the most ambitious plans propose a Council or Parliament of Industry as an administrative headpiece to these sectional bodies, 'to be approved by the Board of Trade'[2] and 'to recommend to the Government'[3] changes in legislation which seem desirable to industry.

The above citations make no pretence of giving the details of the typical schemes now being pressed; but their general trend is unmistakable. Much could, no doubt, be said of the good intentions behind them; but a little ought perhaps to be added *sotto voce* about the awkward political and economic problems which they raise—problems of the democratic control of the powerful economic groups which they would create, remote as these are intended to be from Parliament; problems of the efficient and economical administration of entire industries chartered as monopolies and deprived of the guidance and spur of the competitive market; problems finally—and certainly not least important—of the danger of collusion between labour and management within each group to secure themselves at the expense of the consumer.

On the last point it is not to be thought that an open breach between economic interests can *always* be avoided

1 'Employment Policy and Organization of Industry after the War', Nuffield College, Oxford, 1943, p. 47.

2 'Report of the Association of British Chambers of Commerce', already quoted.

3 The Statement of 120 Business Men, already quoted.

by the device of the green table. When the terms of the economic bargain can no longer be settled by group negotiation, the alternative is not a renewal of the competitive struggle on a thousand fronts, but a pitched battle between huge national organizations of labour and capital, in which the original protestations of devotion to the public service are conveniently forgotten, while the economic life of society itself may be brought nearly to a standstill. If these embarrassing situations become too frequent, no doubt relief is always to be had—on terms—by some kind of dictatorship of the Right or the Left, which could disregard one or other of the special interests and would almost certainly forbid strikes and lockouts, whatever its political complexion. In view of recent events, this solution does not seem a very attractive one. Moreover, the pressure groups, of different kinds of property-owners or of different classes of labour, would still be there, though not so obviously. And the administrative morass of a completely planned economy would form a congenial happy hunting-ground for them.

UNEXPECTED CONVERTS

It seems at first sight odd that proposals which, in principle at least, constitute a standing threat to the democratic way of life should make such a strong appeal to democratic parties of the Left as well as of the Right. The conclusion is perhaps inescapable that on the political principles of the Corporate State, tired business men with no fundamental belief in their own position in society, and tired radicals who have lost their early vision of the equalitarian millennium, can safely and easily unite. The former hope, with considerable historical justification, that in practice they will be able to reach a compromise with the politicians favourable to their interests; the latter, with more logic on their side, hope that in practice it will be easy to squeeze out the business men by constitutional means and restore Paradise by stealth. It is only the discredited but unrepentant minority who think they see in this unnatural union between two opposing interests at the same time the most striking and most threatening phenomenon of modern democratic politics.

What may certainly be called a climax of inappropriateness has, however, been reached in recent times by the aid which this strange political combination has received from two supporters not often found in the same company—namely, Natural Science and the Church. There is, of course, no reason in principle why Churchmen in particular, like other citizens, should not express views on political and economic questions. The support of any political programme by the Church as a corporate body, however, has not had a very happy history in this country, and many Churchmen themselves see dangers in this course. Moreover, the interpretation by individuals of the Divine Will on controversial economic questions, as when a Welsh deputation assured the Minister of Labour in 1936 that the Unemployment Assistance Regulations were contrary to the Christian faith, sometimes provokes doubtless unworthy suspicions that political capital is being made out of the susceptibility of the superstitious. On the whole, and especially in view of the history of religious struggles in this country, the conclusion seems to be that the odds are against a successful mixture of politics and theology and that Churchmen with a political message ought to be constantly on their guard.

Unfortunately, and perhaps inevitably, high Church functionaries who have thought much about social affairs in the recent past, have reached the point in some cases where indignation clouds the understanding and wild shots in the dark are accepted as a good substitute for judgement based on a knowledge of the facts. The Bishop who drew a horrific picture of 'the Bank of England bossing the country and the Empire',[1] and the Archbishop who suggested the reduction of tariffs on imports till they equalized costs,[2] and the 'withering away' of capital after the payment of interest equal to the original sum invested,[3] could not have made a very deep study of the history and theory of the matters under discussion. Similarly, the recommendation of the Archbishop of York's Conference at Malvern[4] calling for a revival of agriculture, the earth to be treated 'no longer as a reservoir of potential wealth to be exploited but as a storehouse of divine bounty on which we utterly depend', seems to be neglectful of the effect of such a revival on the export trades, on which—on a purely secular view, of course—we may be said to depend just as utterly.

Doubtless these are small matters of detail in which the misguided enthusiasms of the Church are not of great moment. But it is a little difficult to be equally charitable with criticisms from the same source directed against the profit motive, the competitive system, and the institution of private property, if they are similarly ill-informed. When the Archbishop called for 'a revival of something like the medieval gilds on the basis of national charters' or for a Planning Authority 'fashioned on the model of the National Joint Industrial Council but expanded so as to be generally representative of industry', the secular planners

[1] The Bishop of Bradford, in a speech to the Socialist Union of Leeds University.

[2] 'Christianity and the Social Order', by the Archbishop of Canterbury, London, 1942, p. 85. Cf. Chapter 6, p. 69.

[3] Op. cit., p. 83. Most lending would immediately cease, and 'capitalistic'—i.e., 'round about'—production would come to an abrupt end with repercussions of some seriousness on the standard of living.

[4] 'The Life of the Church and the Order of Society', Report of the Archbishop of York's Conference at Malvern, 1941.

of the industrial world may no doubt feel gratified that they are in such exalted company; and the unregenerate and worldly-wise amongst them may well find a certain piquant satisfaction in contemplating proposals made by selfish economic interests in their own material interest, which are found on the highest examination to provide one of the essential Christian conditions for the building of an economic Heaven on earth. It may be doubted whether this strange paradox is lost upon the unbeliever; it may be hoped that it is not lost upon the faithful either, and that they may seek to inform themselves on the true issues in these matters.

For the natural scientists there is much less excuse. No one, of course, objects to the application to social problems of the standard scientific method—that is, the formulation of tentative 'laws' about natural phenomena based on accurate observation and the rules of logic; though it is arguable that this method alone would not carry us very far. Nor does anyone deny to scientists, any more than to other citizens, the right to their own views about what society is for, and to what extent, in performing its functions, it should take into account the opinions of the citizens about what they themselves are for. There is, however, no particular reason why the views of professors of physics should, by virtue of their special knowledge of physics, be accorded any more weight on the question of whether conscription is the highest form of democracy,[1] or whether zip fasteners were introduced too late,[2] or whether private enterprise in business is desirable, than the views of eminent divines on the level of the bank rate or the views of eminent film stars on the merits of cigarettes and soap. These

[1] 'Science and World Order', *Transactions of a Conference of the Division for the Social and International Relations of Science*, British Association for the Advancement of Science, London, 1942, p. 9.

[2] 'Science and World Order', p. 16.

personal details have, no doubt, a mild entertainment value because people have always been interested in the eccentricities of the great. But to attribute any higher importance to them would be quite unwarranted.

In practice, however, this mistake is frequently made; and in fact a large and lucrative branch of the advertising profession has been founded on the observed and somewhat astonishing truth that a famous name can be hired to boost anything successfully, from Stock Exchange securities to headache powders, and that the remoteness of the eminent person's life from the product being sold is not of the least consequence. The mixed quality of scientific opinions on social problems is a sobering thought in this connexion. Natural scientists, particularly physicists, chemists, and engineers, have not always had the most suitable training for the study of social and economic phenomena, and the use of their exact, quantitative methods in this field has not infrequently issued in startling new truths akin to the Platonic discovery that a just ruler is 729 times as happy as an unjust one. But this has not restrained them in the past [1]; and in recent years they have been moved to take a closer interest in social affairs by what looks like an odd combination of indignation at the disordered state of the world and a certain shamefacedness at the part taken by their profession in the outcome of the disorder. Certainly the chaotic condition of social and economic affairs during the last twenty years could hardly escape unfavourable comparison with the relatively neat and tidy world of natural science. It is therefore not surprising that scientists, when confronted at their annual conferences with economic problems which have seemed insoluble for generations,

[1] Cf. Hayek, 'Scientism and the Study of Society', *Economica*, February 1943. This article and those by the same author on 'The Counter-Revolution of Science', *Economica*, February, May, and August 1941, are very suggestive on the subject.

should decide that the business of providing for people's material wants is, after all, nothing but an engineering problem of a rather large order; and that the solution is to introduce the Technocratic Paradise, where the Technocrats —namely, the scientific specialists in each industry—set down the scientifically determined needs of the average consumer (which usually bear no recognizable relation to what anybody ever actually wants), multiply by the number of the population, and employ the best technical methods (with a blind eye on costs) to produce the resultant quantities. Numerous scientists of the school of Haldane, Hogben, Bernal, Huxley, and others [1] appear to believe that this procedure is, and always has been, the function of science,[2] that the search for truth for its own sake is impossible, or if possible undesirable, and that the dictatorship of the proletariat is merely a precursor of the dictatorship of the technocrats. It is no accident that most scientists who have given some cursory attention to economic problems conclude that a completely planned economy is the obvious shape of things to come and inquire impatiently what all the fuss of the last two hundred years has been about.

The view that economic activity is devoted to solving a technical problem and that it ought therefore to be directed by technicians is of course a little naïve. It rests on a complete neglect of the fact that technology can take no account of the limitation of resources, which is the dominant reality of the economic world, and on a sublime disregard of the political problem of reconciling the divergent views and interests of those who will have to co-operate in using the resources. The disquieting aspect of the situation is that scientific opinion on economic problems, like religious

[1] Cf. J. D. Bernal, 'Social Functions of Science'; L. Hogben, 'Science for the Citizen'.

[2] Polanyi, 'Growth of Thought in Society', *Economica*, November 1941, refutes this view successfully as regards the past.

opinion, shines with the reflected glory of achievements in a different field; and that both the bishops and the physicists proclaim views about the way economic activity should be organized which, if put into practice, could only lead to various disguised forms of restrictionism in the first place and various forms of political dictatorship ultimately. The restrictionist interests of the business world, who can now appear on the platform with Righteousness on their right hand and Reason on their left, may almost be excused if the eminence of their supporters causes them to fall victim to their own propaganda.

III. THE YEARS TO COME

CHAPTER 8

THE POLITICAL ECONOMY OF FREEDOM

THE pre-war world of Chapters 2–7 was no doubt a wicked world in the sense that growing evils were deliberately ignored. But candour requires the admission for the benefit of the thoughtful and sorely perplexed minority who had to live in it that it was also a most bewildering one. In the circumstances the charitable view is perhaps that there is no excuse for people who deceive *themselves*. (And by that common failing, it may be added, how many of the mighty were brought low in those years and how much and how long we all suffered for it!) It may well be that whatever standards of value survive into the post-war world, the one unforgivable sin in the eyes of a generation which has suffered from two world wars will be self-deception—at least within the narrow scope of the matters discussed in this book.

The particular blind spot of the interventionist mentality during the inter-war period was not only its failure to appreciate the economic losses of restrictionism, but also its inability to see the threat to the continuance of political freedom which Government interventions on the massive scale of that period implied. From the point of view of practical statesmanship the first error was a typical piece of self-deception, and involved a needless diminution in the standard of living of a poverty-stricken world; but the second was disastrous, and threatened the quality of life itself. Amongst governments accustomed to proclaim their devotion to democratic and liberal ideals this is a saddening combination of errors.

It is, of course, not surprising that the sudden and drastic economic changes to which people had to accustom themselves after 1918 produced a sense of insecurity to which restrictionism on the part of those groups for whom it was possible seemed from the first the easy and obvious answer. Governments themselves had no alternative one. Indeed, at a time of economic earthquakes the advantages of Peace and Quiet in the haven of an officially sponsored monopoly can be very effectively demonstrated to harassed politicians burdened by over-generous election promises. And it is an easy step for these to conclude that if only all industries were similarly organized, the earthquakes could be disregarded. Nevertheless, only the most incorrigible optimist outside the Administration (and perhaps a handful of loyal Civil servants as well) could survey the economic patchwork of 1919–39 and say that it was good. The problems of post-war reconstruction were then unprecedented and must have appeared formidable; but the tragic mixture of good intentions, surrenders to vested interests, and sheer official muddling characteristic of the solutions applied, does not give much confidence that they were the right ones.

The drastic economic changes of twenty-five years ago will recur, with differences mainly of degree. In due time, at the end of the ambulance period when people have been helped on to their economic feet, it is only too likely that complicated problems of re-adapting the industrial structure will again confront us. Again we may choose the easy and obvious ways of helping lame dogs over the stile; again we shall find that in practice this means Government help and approval for various complicated ways of producing less and getting paid more for it; and again we shall see the inevitable accompaniment of more and more 'delegated legislation', with the Governments responsible for it coming still further under the equivocal influence of sectional economic interests strong enough to be troublesome. The question whether all this is inevitable, and if it is, how long the democratic system will stand the strain, seems in the circumstances natural enough.

THE HISTORICAL TREND

The question has uncomfortable implications, the chief of which is the appropriateness of a political and economic system in the coming years which is incomprehensively at variance with historical trend. The rules of conduct for men living in society have, it is true, been very variously formulated since the dawn of reason. But the tendency of Western thought, at least, has been to frame them against a philosophical background of the respect which is due to the individual personality from other individuals and from the State, and to harmonize them with the long history of the emancipation of individual men from the spiritual thraldom of any particular body of religious beliefs which they do not freely accept from their own inner convictions, and from the political thraldom of any particular form of government which they do not freely choose themselves. The emphasis has been on an ever-widening sphere of free choice in thought and action for every individual citizen on an equal basis, and on successive retreats of the State from the business of enforcing the good life on its citizens. It has now come to be widely believed in civilized society that in all the important decisions of life the sphere of compulsion from without is limited by its complete inability to achieve its own ends. The flowering of the human spirit cannot be forced. The moral stature of individual man can increase only in proportion as he becomes more and more responsible for his own acts.

It is not without significance in this connexion that the case for *religious* freedom is nowadays taken almost everywhere for granted. 'Ought', says modern man, following Kant, has no meaning except for those who 'can'. This particular battle was fought and won decisively centuries ago. *Political* liberties, the liberty of thought and speech and equality before the law, are not, it is true, completely secure in some countries at present. But the second World War was fought to restore them; and they are being restored. It seems thus at first sight a little odd that *economic* liberties should have come to be increasingly restricted before the present war and should seem likely to be denied altogether after it.

Up to the latter part of the nineteenth century the contradiction was not outwardly apparent. Political freedom won its victories almost hand in hand with economic freedom. But the philosophers of the movement had really spoilt a good case by over-rationalizing it. The idea of the Social Contract, expounded by Rousseau in France and John Locke in England, representing Man originally free but bargaining away some of his 'natural rights' in return for good government, is no doubt far from the puerile misunderstanding of history which subsequent critics have represented it to be. But it provides no precise answer to the crucial question—on what principle can the State override the 'natural rights' of individuals in cases of conflict? Bentham's answer, that State intervention is justified whenever it can be shown to produce the greatest happiness of the greatest number, held the field for almost the whole of the nineteenth century. But, as Sidgwick and others pointed out, it involves an objective measure of happiness applicable to all, which is inconceivable. The result was that the twentieth century inherited nothing but a good moral tradition and two elaborate philosophical systems in ruins.

The moral tradition is evidently vital. The grand argument for the sanctity of the individual personality, which is the moral basis of a régime of individual freedom, hardly needs to be retraced by any pedestrian philosophical pen. It is not on this level of discourse that the faint hearts of our own time, wondering dejectedly whether people really want to be free, can get their courage up. Those who have not heard the majestic voices ringing down the ages—and not the Christian voices only—are not likely to be converted by the somewhat humdrum music of eighteenth- and nineteenth-century philosophy. Freedom is ultimately a question for the imagination, not the intellect.

Nevertheless, the philosophical ruins were a disaster. The ideals of political freedom were intact. But without a coherent philosophy of freedom, political action was hamstrung. Moreover, the ruins involved a substantial part of classical economics. During the seventy years between Adam Smith and John Stuart Mill, the economic implications of a régime of individual liberty received their most finished exposition in the light of the conditions of that time. But intellectual allegiance to the classical system was severely shaken by criticisms of the Benthamite philosophy on which it was based. And the system was not only defective in itself at some points; it was also very inadequately reflected in law and in business practice. Distinct signs of what, from the point of view of this system, may be called the degeneration of capitalism, set in towards the close of the nineteenth century.

The degeneration was the work of many uncomprehending but well-meaning hands. The earliest and chief error was to allow the private manufacture of money. The money system, by which purchasing power is generalized and men are released from an intolerable dependence on barter, is certainly one of the most important inventions in world history, and it has led to a vast extension of the freedom of individual choice between different goods in the present and between goods in the present and goods in the future. Its abuse in private hands has probably been the chief inflammatory agent, if not the main cause of booms and slumps. A mistake of comparable importance was to allow the glaring inequalities of wealth to develop which were common at the end of last century, and which were the inevitable results of the operation of the contemporary free market. These inequalities were accompanied by extreme concentration of economic power which still exists, and which threatens the entire system.

Errors of this sort resulted from the very successes of capitalism, which produced an almost superstitious reverence for its early forms, and for the opinions of the often disagreeable persons who were its brightest products a hundred years ago. As the standard of living under free conditions advanced at a rate which outstripped even the phenomenal increase in population, *all* State intervention became suspect, and from Ricardo to Herbert Spencer the most extreme positions on this front were defended by the most eminent. After the first World War, the errors, though more glaring, were of quite the opposite kind. Economic freedom was then under a cloud. The burden of proof had slowly shifted from those who wished to restrict freedom to those who wished to retain it. There came the decades of well-intentioned muddling between the wars which, contrary to all intention, almost succeeded in obliterating the principal operating parts of the capitalist machine altogether.

This is a tragic tale of the disappointment of reasonable hopes. The first part of the nineteenth century had seen a real promise of the economic emancipation of the Common Man, whose spiritual and material freedoms had been slowly expanding, though with many setbacks, for generations past. Since about 1870 the performance of the economic system failed to live up to the promise. Tremendous disparities of wealth brought back inequalities of power in an almost feudal form, and periodical business crises left a trail of hardship and poverty which made economic freedom seem just as illusory to the industrial proletariat as it had been to their peasant ancestors centuries before. There was no clear voice explaining why this should be, but only the tiresome and repetitious incantation of century-old dogmas. The workers and their employers, farmers, business men, shopkeepers—turned to politics in disgust; and the centre of the economic struggle gradually shifted from the market-place to Westminster and Whitehall.

If the lunatic years of the inter-war period are any guide, this desperate remedy is not without its drawbacks. Governments are seen to consist of fallible and vulnerable men and their machinery sometimes clumsy and ill-adapted to run in harness with the patched-up and choked-up engines of capitalism. The game of politics is revealed as no more respectable, and perhaps even less difficult for the cheats, than the game of business. In the political arena, the unnatural behaviour of the lions of business, who for some strange reason appear to be on the best of terms with one another, is a constant source of perplexity to the ingenuous and of suspicion to the critics. The magnanimous amongst the former, gratified at what is perhaps a change of heart, now regard the king of beasts as a reformed character and press even more powers upon him. Others, remembering his former crimes, call loudly for his destruction, though the low forms of life with which they wish to replace him are not universally popular. More realistic critics are beginning to ask themselves whether the retreat from the market-place was not perhaps too precipitous. But they seem to face a grim choice. If restrictionism and all its works is rejected, the uninviting alternatives appear to lie between the crude capitalism of the nineteenth century, when some enjoyed freedom of choice and used it to exploit others and destroy the system, and the Corporate State of the twentieth century, when economic freedom, and ultimately other freedoms, too, are sacrificed for a variety of ends to which individual choices are subordinate.

THE BASIC CONDITIONS OF FREEDOM

The choice, though still a hard one, is in fact not quite so grim as this. There is another alternative. It is to think through again the political economy of a free society in the light of nineteenth-century experience and of modern economic conditions, and to survey again the institutional requirements of an economic system where all choices are accessible to all men so long as the system which ensures freedom of choice is not itself endangered.

Thoughts on this subject in the past have ensured their unpopularity with modern audiences by taking the form of a system of *negative* rules governing action by the State, as for example the very sensible maxim which forbids the State to make continuous grants of special favours or privileges to sectional economic interests. But there is no reason why some of the thunder should not be stolen from the twentieth-century interventionists in this matter and an adequate institutional framework for the free economy set down as a *positive* and *continuing* care of the State. The task can be conveniently described in a concise and appropriately provocative form of words—that *the primary if not the sole economic function of the State is to maintain the free market.*

The free market, which is merely a simple practical device for giving effect to individual choice, is the very heart of the free economic system, and the widest possible extension of this device is the best guarantee of economic freedom. In their efforts to justify these claims, however, economists have perhaps too often relied upon mysterious symbols and esoteric arguments in technical language which have seemed to prove much more than they did. In ordinary language, the economic case claims that the machinery of the market in registering the free choices of buyers and sellers generates pressures which tend to move every productive resource into that position in the economic system where it can make the largest possible addition to the income of the community (measured in terms of price), and generates rewards for each participant in production which tend to equal the increase in the community's income which his co-operation makes possible.

This sort of recitation always irritates the sceptics, who with a certain justification look askance at an argument which seems to prove not only that the free market brings about the most efficient production, but that it pays everyone his deserts. In fact, however, suspicion is needless. The claims actually made are exceedingly modest, and in the brief formulation of them in the previous paragraph there are concealed assumptions which reduce the whole to a very small nub of essential truth indeed.

In the first place, the choices of buyers and sellers are free only in a rather superficial sense. In these days of gigantic advertising appropriations and high-pressure salesmanship, it is becoming difficult to overlook the fact that people's wants are to a large extent manufactured by the productive system itself along with the commodities necessary to satisfy them. In the second place, all buyers do not start from scratch. Large sections of the market where most people would like to buy but cannot afford to, are dominated by the rich. Some inequality of this sort is, indeed, an inevitable accompaniment of free market operations, because sellers are better rewarded for furnishing things that are more wanted than they are for things that are less wanted. But those who do not happen to be rich commonly find the inequalities in practice so glaring that it seems sometimes as if the market is rigged against them. They may claim that if rewards were made more equal by transfers from the rich, who would not feel the loss as much as the poor feel the gain, everybody would enter the market on more equal terms.

To this objection to inequality, the only answer is that ' feelings ' of loss or gain are not measurable as between individuals, and that therefore the case for redistribution must be regarded as not proven. But this line of argument (which was used against the Benthamites) removes yet a third prop from the case for the free market, for if satisfactions cannot be measured, the conception of the ' income of the community ', which the operation of the free market is said to maximize, can only be given an arbitrary meaning. Further, the maximum is reached only where there is completely free entry to the market for anyone who thinks he has a chance of selling what is wanted at a profit. Of course, free entry by itself will not ensure that the most efficient or most suitable sellers will enter, or indeed that anyone will enter at all. Starting business in some lines may be particularly risky or expensive, so that perhaps only one entrant will be found willing to take the risk, and even he may come in only on the understanding that the Government keeps everyone else out. More generally, owners of particularly scarce property or scarce labour are not *obliged* to hire or sell them out. Even if the market price is favourable, they may merely choose to pay a money penalty for not doing so. Thus a free market does not necessarily produce what many people would call a rich society. Farmers in England *may* choose to stay on the land though they could earn more money as mechanics.

We are therefore left with the rather modest conclusion that if the act of choice is rational and well-informed, which is unusual, if buyers and sellers start from scratch, which is contrary to experience, if each man can be assumed to get the same satisfaction out of a penny spent from a given income, which is highly debatable, and if the market is in fact free to all comers, which is the opposite of what most people have wanted for the last twenty years, then we may say that economic freedom is the most beneficial system conceivable for society as a whole.[1]

Plainly this is but an uncertain key to the best of all possible worlds. Worse still, it makes a very unconvincing exhibit at election times. Nothing is easier, in fact, than to show that the free market works imperfectly, and that under other equally arbitrary assumptions unconnected with individual freedom, alternative systems of production varying from communism to brigandage and alternative systems of distribution varying from charity to everybody taking what they like, would produce superior results. When it is viewed against the practical alternatives, however, and particularly the alternatives of Chapters 2–7, certain essentially humble but useful qualities of the free market seem to have some claim on the attention of practical men.

The free market widens choice; and the extension of choice increases economic freedom. The market is internally consistent—that is to say, given the wants of buyers and sellers as they are, the market will discourage the retention of resources in any use if it is clear that they could be better employed elsewhere.[2] The market is

[1] There are numerous other but less important imperfections. Thus there is an implicit assumption of mobility, homogeneity, and divisability of economic goods, and of rational foresight on the part of economic subjects. Cf. e.g., F. Knight, 'Ethics of Competition', London, 1935, pp. 49–57.

[2] This advantage is so crucial in a highly complex economic system that Socialist economists have made a very strong case for retaining a kind of synthetic competitive market in the Socialist State. Cf. Lange, 'Economic Theory of Socialism', Minneapolis, 1938.

impersonal, and no single individual is responsible for its results—a virtue of immense practical importance. In democratic politics there is the well-known golden rule that when things go wrong, there must always be somebody to hang—i.e., somebody to answer questions in the House of Commons. Economic affairs are far too serious for such polite arrangements. If things go wrong in the interventionist State, it is only too likely that parsimonious price-fixers will in fact be hanged by infuriated sellers, and still more likely that parsimonious wage-fixers will be hanged by infuriated workers. The market substitutes general rules for particular and local expedients; it dissipates economic responsibilities and keeps them out of politics; it breaks up the tremendous struggles between huge and highly organized interests which periodically shake the foundations of ordered society, and substitutes competition 'on a thousand fronts'. The market is the nurse of material progress and the forcing-house of economic development. The right to 'shop around' is the best practical guarantee that buyers and sellers will get what they really want. Though the planners may produce schemes which are faultless in logic and are miracles of ingenuity on paper, it is contrary to all the promptings of common sense to suppose that any safeguard against the exploitation of one individual by another could be devised for the economic sphere which is superior in practice to the simple right to patronize the rival shop at will.

These arguments can hardly be described as beyond the comprehension of anyone who has spent a Saturday afternoon shopping, and the advantages they suggest for the shopper are, in fact, normally taken for granted. There are probably few of this numerous and hardy band who have not reflected at some time or other as they retired from the last counter with unexpectedly little change that there would be something to be said for a really free market, and that the substitute offered in 1939 by professional politicians, only too prone to promise all things to all men (who can reach them), or by bureaucrats, only too anxious not to offend any man, was not particularly acceptable. There are, it is true, unreliable salesmen just as there are unreliable politicians. But the salesman is more easily, more promptly and more often found out.

Of course, no one—and certainly not the comfort-loving Captain of modern industry—dreams of returning to the ungentlemanly crudities of early nineteenth-century capitalism. Nineteenth-century experience shows clearly that the advantages of a free market cannot be secured by allowing every participant to do as he likes, and present-day opinion indicates that they can be made acceptable only if some attempt is made to meet the criticisms set out above. Here is evidently the proper occasion for the intervention of the State in building and maintaining a framework of general rules, applicable to all alike and conceived in the light of the principle that restraints on the freedom of some are justified only if there is a threat to the freedom of all. The rules will not be invariable from time to time or from country to country, since their content depends essentially on such imponderables as how much people will stand from their Governments at a time, how they would behave in the absence of rules, and who could be entrusted with enforcement. But the following paragraphs will show their general direction and the problems which must be solved before they can be applied.

ACCESS TO INFORMATION

The act of choice of buyer and seller in a free market is the supreme economic act. Buying an apple for a penny is the culminating stage of a long and complicated process into which much hard work and anxious thought have gone. Buyer and seller ought therefore to be surrounded with all necessary safeguards, so that they can make the most of their market opportunities. Thus the Government must guarantee public order, so that markets may be established and choice can be deliberate; and it must provide an educational system, so that choice can be informed and meaningful. However unfortunate it might seem from some points of view, the latter condition does not mean the universal teaching of economic theory to the mystified and uncomprehending young. It does mean that the young must learn, each according to his individual capacity, about the economic facts of the world and the alternatives of conduct in relation to them. There is an unanswerable economic case for equality of educational opportunity at the start of the race. A free market in which the range of knowledge and experience of the buyers and sellers depends on the accident of birth does not make sense. And there is considerable ground for thinking that if there was less educational inequality at the beginning of the race, there would be less economic inequality at the end of it.

The results of the failure to measure up to the educational requirements of the free system are obvious to all, though the causes are often mistaken. The depravity of taste in modern capitalistic societies is not due to the fact that life is 'over-commercialized', but to the fact that life is not commercialized enough. The range of personal desires of the average citizen is pitifully narrow; and it is not surprising that those who do not know how life could be lived, live it so meanly. It is not the market which should be blamed for offering in cheap profusion the showy trivialities which are the characteristic products of the modern age, but the tragic and avoidable ignorance of those who demand such things.

The informative side of the educational process ought therefore to be continued throughout life. The adult citizen particularly needs information, or knowledge of where to get information, on employment, consumption, and investment prospects. In modern countries he is singularly ill-served in respect of all of these requirements. Either the information does not exist, or it is incomplete, wrong, or given in a way which leads to all kinds of unnecessary wastes. The lack of proper information in practice slows down market adjustments, prevents an equilibrium from being reached rapidly, or reached at all, permits various wasteful discriminations between different buyers and sellers, and leads people to waste their substance on goods and on activities they would avoid if they knew the facts. Of course, a large part of economic activity nowadays is normally directed to providing market information, in the form of advertisements. But no one with the smallest powers of observation could fail to be struck by the fact that advertisements are not invariably distinguished by a strict adherence to the truth. And the information they do give is normally much diluted by 'pure' salesmanship, or irrational appeals to buy irrespective of merits. This is largely the fault of the educational system, which in this country is insufficiently focused on the problem of economic choice, and which in general proceeds in sublime disregard of the economic realities which the young are expected to cope with unaided on leaving school. One of the most depressing consequences of this is the development of successful advertising techniques based on the principle that so long as adult consumers can be got to recognize a brand name on a packet, the less they are told about the contents that has any relation to its merits the more they will buy it.

We are here confronted with what seems at first sight the characteristic dilemma of social action. The job is the apparently simple one of informing people what they can work at and what they can do with what they get for their work. The free system as we know it does the job with very unequal success in different parts of the economic field. In particular, advertisements to consumers are a revolting mixture of lies, half-truths, and spell-binding irrelevancies; and the wastes involved in building up brand names and reputations by competitive advertising are very large. Experience shows that the most outrageous deceptions can be practised on the long-suffering public for an indefinite time before they are found out, and that in consequence an unnecessarily large part of the productive machine is turned over to the making of things that sell well in place of others, equally desired, which do not.

But the alternative of salesmanship by collective action is worse. For it means ultimately that the Government will have to be granted the power to set arbitrary limits to the area of free choice. The temptation would be to assume, as many a good bureaucrat might, that no respectable citizen could possibly want more than three buttons down his waistcoat, or, as an ambitious politician might, that no right-minded patriot should prefer foreign-produced butter to the home variety, or either to guns. No doubt the purely informative side of the business could be usefully done by the Government, or, better still, by buyers and sellers themselves acting under conditions imposed by Government. Further, where the qualities of goods can be tested, and the tests are quite objective, as for the chemical composition of paint or the technical performance of refrigerators, there is, no doubt, something to be said for some Government body applying the tests and communicating the results to consumers. But to make an elected Government the arbiter of consumers' choice in any way, and particularly for individual commodities, is the beginning of collective madness. The right way to proceed is the slow, difficult, and laborious way of implanting sound criteria of choice in the mind of the consumer while he is educable, and ensuring that he is supplied afterwards, at his desire, with full and correct information about the markets he is active in.[1] So far as the act of choice itself is concerned, there is no reliable substitute for individual responsibility.

One of the most attractive advantages of a completely planned economy is that its business enterprises operate 'within glass walls'—that is, everybody responsible for important economic decisions knows what everybody else is up to. Conversely, a fundamental weakness of the competitive system as operated at present is the ignorance of the individual enterpriser about the doings of his competitors. Now, it cannot be denied that the collection of the economic information which would meet this need has often been done in the past by individual enthusiasts who were chiefly distinguished by a human but regrettable weakness for marrying unwarrantable assumptions and foregone conclusions. No one should wish to restrain these efforts. But the main business of continuous economic reporting is a function which could well be performed by the Government. In practice it is likely that a very fair approximation to the economy of the glass walls could be reached if the Government would collect and publish the maximum information about developments in all branches of economic activity, so that those concerned would know what was happening around them in their own affairs and could keep the attractions and drawbacks of other activities beside their own constantly before them.

LIMITATIONS TO INEQUALITIES OF WEALTH

Even if people knew what to choose from, the unhampered operation of the pricing system would under present conditions produce the most extraordinary economic anomalies, because all buyers and sellers do not start from scratch. Extremes of wealth and poverty, though now less

[1] This line of argument is further developed in the author's 'Advertising Reconsidered', London, 1935.

than they were, are still so great that for large numbers of people economic freedom seems nominal. Moreover, even if everybody did start from scratch, differences of capacity (not to speak of luck) between individuals would be reflected in gross inequalities of wealth at an early stage. Gross inequalities, whether of income or of accumulated wealth, have the effect of rigging the market. The control of resources comes to be concentrated in few hands, the purity of politics is endangered, and attempts are bound to be made sooner or later, in the name of justice for particular under-dogs, to offset the advantages of superior wealth by price-fixing, sectional restrictionist devices, and other highly dubious arrangements for interfering with the operation of the machinery which offers the only hope of practicable distributive justice—namely, the free market. No one is likely to think himself free while there are multi-millionaires, unless he happens to be one. No one whose income depends on working less and getting more for it is likely to suffer from a particularly bad conscience before a fellow-citizen who draws a thousand times as much from a perfectly blameless competitive source.

The most obvious and least defensible inequalities are those of property ownership. According to the calculations of Campion,[1] based on necessarily arbitrary definitions of 'property' and 'ownership', 1 per cent of the persons aged twenty-five and over in England and Wales owned more than half of the total property in private hands in 1936. On the other hand, in 1936 three-quarters of the adult persons in England and Wales owned little more than 5 per cent of the total property in private hands. No one interested in the extension of economic freedom is entitled to draw much comfort from these figures, though the indications are that the inequalities which they measure are

[1] 'Public and Private Property in Great Britain', H. Campion, London, 1939, p. 109.

decreasing, as a consequence of increasingly heavy death duties. The rate of death duties before the war varied from approximately 20 per cent on estates of £100,000–£200,000 to 50 per cent on estates of £2,000,000 and over; and the recent increases have been so steep that it is now almost literally true that the rich would be better off if they had less property and were therefore worse off—i.e., the annual burden of death duties on an investment income of £50,000 had increased by 1941–2 to 108 per cent, or more than the income.[1] Nevertheless it is still glaringly obvious that ownership of property gives a running start. John Stuart Mill's classical lament on these matters is hard to beat and impossible to answer: 'The principle of private property has never yet had a fair trial in any country. . . . The laws of property have never yet conformed to the principles on which the justification of private property rests. . . . They have not held the balance fairly between human beings but have heaped impediments on some, to the advantage of others; they have purposely fostered inequalities and prevented all from starting fair in the race.'[2]

Inequalities of property ownership are a major cause of inequalities of income. Very large incomes normally show a high proportion of 'unearned' income from property. The Chancellor's recent figures for income-tax payers throw a lurid light on the inequalities of income for this class in 1938.[3] 105,000 people in the top class, earning over £2,000 a year, made £530 millions—nearly as much as the £590 millions made by the 1,750,000 people in the bottom class, earning £250–£500 a year. At the lower

[1] The calculation is based on the assumption that property-owners desire their estates to be transmitted intact and free of death duties—which equalitarians will claim it is the very object of the death duties to prevent. Cf. 'The Burden of British Taxation', Shirras and Rostas, Cambridge, 1942, p. 77.

[2] 'Principles', pp. 208–9.

[3] House of Commons Debates, 23 July 1942.

end of the general income scale, Orr's admittedly rough estimates of pre-war incomes by income groups, based on wage rates in particular occupations, suggest that as much as 10 per cent of the population had incomes of 10*s.* a week per head or less.[1]

As in the case of property ownership, so in the case of income, the inequalities between individuals are being lessened by taxation. The pre-war burden of direct and indirect taxation on the earned income of a single man has been computed at 57 per cent of an income of £50,000, 39 per cent of £10,000, 15 per cent of £1,000, and 4 per cent of £100.[2]

Contrary to the popular view, encouraged by reformers in a hurry, the reduction of inequalities is not simply a problem of how to plunder the rich most rapidly and most effectively. It is a problem of how to prevent the free market from being destroyed by the unhindered operation of the forces which it generates. For guidance something more is required than the homely Treasury maxim to spare the goose that lays the golden eggs, and the best general rule seems to be that any necessary redistribution of wealth and income should be carried out with the minimum of distortion of prices in general and of the rewards and incentives for enterprise and accumulation in particular.

Obviously this is a counsel of perfection. In the case of

[1] 'Food, Health, and Income', J. B. Orr, London, 1936, p. 60.

Population of Great Britain by Income Groups

Income per head per week	Estimated Population	% of Total Population
Up to 10*s.*	4,500,000	10%
10*s.* to 15*s.*	9,000,000	20%
15*s.* to 20*s.*	9,000,000	20%
20*s.* to 30*s.*	9,000,000	20%
30*s.* to 45*s.*	9,000,000	20%
Over 45*s.*	4,500,000	10%

[2] Shirras and Rostas, op. cit., p. 47.

income redistribution, price distortion is bound to be considerable. For example, on the assumption that the rich acquire at least a part of their riches by particular sorts of work directed to that end, then any tax on inequality will discriminate against those sorts of work. But some of the grosser kinds of distortion can easily be identified and avoided. Thus a considerable redistribution of income can be and is brought about by restriction of production in particular lines. Apart from the fact that this in general involves a transfer from the poor, who are not so good at it, to the rich, who can form producers' monopolies more easily, it is clear that such transfers could be brought about at less cost to the community by producing the maximum and imposing a levy on final incomes in order to finance the transfer. Government fixing of artificially low prices for goods consumed by the poor is another administratively seductive but fundamentally wasteful method of redistribution, because at any but the free price, output is no longer at the most efficient level. It is little advance on this for harassed Governments, eager for the path of economic rectitude, to buy the goods themselves at the free price and supply them to needy consumers at less than cost, for if the consumer had been given the money instead, the odds are that he would have spent it differently. A money transfer is, in fact, the best method. Here is the complete answer to those lovers of humanity who justify public works by claiming that the poor ought to be glad to have things which the Government thinks they ought to want, at prices lower than they would have to pay if they bought in the free market—which *ex hypothesi* they would not. Essentially the same line of argument disposes of any claims which indirect taxes on consumption goods may have as redistributive agents—these taxes make it impossible for consumers to use their incomes most effectively.

The claim of a direct tax on final income to effect an

economical redistribution of income is much superior to that of any of these expedients. But as administered in this country, it still does not satisfy the criterion of minimum price distortion as well as it might.[1] Taxes should not discriminate between the different ways in which people may choose to employ their income—i.e., whether they spend or save it. Present income taxation falls with double weight on saving because there is a levy on income when it is received and also on the fruits of saving out of that income when they are received. But there is no tax at all on capital gains, which constitutes an undue encouragement to flutters on the Stock Exchange. The first of these discriminations can be avoided to some extent by Irving Fisher's proposal for a tax on expenditure rather than on income, though this would leave untouched, at least during their lifetimes, the vast economic empires built up by frugal millionaires, which constitute a special menace to economic freedom.

A more promising line is a complete redefinition of 'income' so as to take account of the change in the taxpayer's whole financial position during the period of assessment.[2] If the definition were to be constructed consistently, it would take account of changes in the taxpayer's accumulated wealth, for example by inheritances during his lifetime, as well as his income. Normally these changes are a distinct and separate target for the tax-gatherer, who by imposing levies on them operates to reduce inequalities of accumulated wealth as distinct from inequalities of income.[3]

[1] Cf. Benham, 'What is the Best Tax System', *Economica*, May 1942.

[2] Proposed in H. Simons, 'Personal Income Taxation', Chicago.

[3] In practice, taxation is not the only way to do this. For instance, Government may take some of the sting out of inequality by curtailing the 'rights' of ownership, or by nationalizing important sections of the economy. The second course had already proceeded far in this

There is no reason why the many ingenious proposals in this field, including Mill's suggestion of a ceiling on individual inheritances, and the Rignano principle of inheritance taxes which are ' progressive in time ', should not be fitted into a comprehensive income tax. The Rignano principle is particularly commendable for its minimum disturbing effect on the free market system. The central idea is that the rate of taxation increases with the number of times the property changes hands through inheritance, so that the burden is a light one on accumulations during the lifetime of the saver, but a heavy one on what he inherits. In this way a given levy on accumulated wealth is raised with the minimum disturbance to the work and savings activity of the individual taxpayer during his own lifetime.

Supposing a good method of redistribution by a comprehensive income tax is found, there is still the question of how far the redistribution should go. The height of the ' ceiling ' for riches is likely to be least troublesome because any reasonable limitation sufficient to prevent rich individuals from interfering with the competitive operation of the market would not be low enough to restrict seriously the rate of accumulation or the incentive to work. The appropriate ' floor ', however, below which the Government should intervene to supplement earnings, is more contentious. Assuming that all start fair in the race, there would be no case for a Government bonus on the normal going wage of unskilled labour. As the opening move in the campaign against inequalities, therefore, it would be the business of the State to see that all did start fair—within reasonable limits. Absolute equality in this matter is not

country before the war and now seems due for a further considerable extension. Both methods involve bargains between the State and particular groups of owners and are therefore politically objectionable. They are remedies of last resort.

possible while the family remains the unit of economic life, and would be undesirable if it were possible. But regardless of family income, each entrant should know what the race is about, what the prizes are, and what sort of efforts are needed to win them. Those who have to be assisted at the training stage after they have made their choice ought to be able to compete for free places at State training centres, or borrow Government money under appropriate conditions to pay for their training.

Given the fair start, however, a sizeable number of people normally fall by the way even in the richest countries, and for reasons of ill-health, bad luck, or various forms of incapacity, fail to earn enough under free conditions to ensure a decent livelihood. For such people the Government must fix a lower earnings limit. Too low a limit would make free choice meaningless. But too high a limit would sap incentive, reduce labour mobility by discouraging people from changing their jobs, and put a premium on long-drawn-out industrial warfare. It is true that the security of guaranteed minimum earnings might induce some people, in whom the spirit of enterprise ran strong, to work harder and take *more* risks in moving from job to job; but it is safer to assume that in the ordinary workaday world, where industrial conditions are always assumed to have the durability of geological epochs and everybody is scandalized when this assumption is upset, such risk-takers would be in a minority. In a rich society the chance of making some of the others lazy by paying them something whether they work or not is considerable, and is perhaps best regarded as one of the quite inevitable costs of getting rich.

It ought not to imply, however, that people are paid periodical sums of money on the strict condition that they bind themselves not to do any work at all. And to prevent this the Government must be prepared not with periodical flat rate payments on the model of the Beveridge plan, but with payments to ' make up ' earnings whenever they fall below a reasonable minimum.[1] Effective competition amongst employers would prevent them from throwing part of their labour costs on to the State by paying less than the market wage, and collusion between employers and workers to defraud the State would probably be no more frequent or costly than income-tax evasion is at present, and could be minimized by much the same machinery. Of course the definition of a reasonable minimum would have to be in practice a somewhat arbitrary compromise between what conservatives thought the community could afford and what radicals thought that people ought to have. But a successful operative minimum which did not lead to restrictions on work would have to take the form of a ' balancing ' money payment, whatever the amount.

THE MONEY SUPPLY

One of the most awkward consequences of the crude nineteenth-century version of economic freedom was the freedom permitted to banks to create money. At first, this meant in practice that banks printed their own notes; and the effect was that streams of new money were added to the circulation when business was good and expenditure already running high, and withdrawn when business was bad and expenditure low, thus exaggerating business fluctuations and producing ruinous waves of bank failures during a slump. The commercial banker, who occupied a very exalted place indeed in the economic hierarchy, thus came near to being the real devil of the piece from the point of view of the disturbing ups and downs of business at that time. Moreover, his influence still remained even after the banks had been deprived of their right of note

[1] R. F. Harrod, ' Full Employment ', *Economic Journal*, December 1943.

issue, since cheques drawn against credits which banks can 'create' by a simple process of bookkeeping, took the place of notes. The fundamental and perverse instability of the monetary circulation was therefore still present.

Nowadays the prestige of the banker as an economic oracle is still quite substantial, but the Government, acting through the Bank of England, has far more control of the situation. If the currency tends to expand at the wrong times, there are effective ways and means of applying the brake, as in 1920, for instance, when a rise in interest rates brought the volume of money in circulation down with a rush. Unfortunately, the Bank of England has no good way of producing the opposite effect—that is, of expanding the circulation during a slump. This is a severe drawback to sensible monetary management, because a prolonged spell of bad business results from a continuing deficiency in the *aggregate* money demand for goods and services, and it is just such a deficiency that a rise in the monetary circulation could supply. The deficiency may start in a small way, even by the failure of some one key concern; but it is turned into a generalized slump by people getting panicky and all trying to liquidate their assets at once. With a given supply of money it is, of course, impossible for all firms to ensure their own solvency at the same time: in fact, any serious attempt to do so merely precipitates a scramble for the available money supply and produces exactly the opposite—that is, insolvency in general.

It is the accompanying hold-up in the monetary circulation, when money which would normally be paid out as wages and other costs of production is withdrawn from active use and hoarded, that causes general slumps. Two conclusions seem clear. First, the private manufacture of money is a good example of one of the economic freedoms the exercise of which can make (and many would add, has made) the functioning of the free system itself impossible.

The creation of a reliable and adequate money supply is the business of the Government. The banks should be effectively prevented from manufacturing money of their own by a legal obligation to keep £1 for £1 reserve against demand deposits.

Second, as soon as there is any danger of a fall in aggregate demand, the Government must stand ready to build up the active money circulation before the general scramble for financial liquidity gets really going. This is the *raison d'être* of public works, consumers' credits, 'Budget balancing over the trade cycle', and other proposals for increasing the money supply as business activity declines. The chief drawback to these methods is that in practice they are very slow. Public works take normally several years between the decision of the responsible authorities and the injection of new money into the circulation. Budgets are presented normally once a year. There is perhaps some hope of varying tax payments month by month or, better still, putting all the financial operations of the Government on a monthly basis. In view of the paramount necessity for speed, however, a scheme for 'commodity currency',[1] somewhat on the following lines, has considerable advantages.

The Government sets up a Stabilization Pool on the lines of the 'buffer stock' schemes advocated for the stabilization of the prices of primary products entering into international trade. The Pool, financed by the creation of new money by the Government, undertakes to buy in large lots any quantity of any commodity figuring on a selected list, the buying price being somewhat below the cost (excluding

[1] What follows is based essentially on the writings of Prof. Frank D. Graham. Cf. especially 'Social Goals and Economic Institutions', Princeton, 1943; 'Full Employment without Public Works', *Quarterly Review of American Labour Conference on International Affairs*, October 1945.

the service of capital) in a normal period, of the most efficient firms in the industry concerned. Goods would be sealed and stored with the producer at his expense. The list would include all commodities made to an identifiable standard or a standard specification, and would thus cover raw materials like coal and pig-iron, semi-fabricated materials like steel plates and industrial chemicals, and a large variety of finished 'utility' goods like clothing, footwear, storeable foods, furniture, and simple household utensils. The longer the list the more widespread the effect of the injections of purchasing power through the Pool operations.

The Pool buying price would set a 'floor' for selected prices, and for other prices, too, as the repercussion of Pool purchases spread throughout the system. When the demand for money to hoard was satisfied (the existence of the floor would restrain hoarding anyway), prices would rise above costs, manufacturers would thus be induced by the prospect of profit to buy back their stocks from the Pool, and activity would rise to normal. Short of a collapse of the currency, business activity would be bound to rise soon after the Pool began priming the pump. Collapse of the currency is inconceivable at the point where the Pool would begin operations, as it is just at that point that holders of goods are most anxious to change their goods into money. Conversely, in case of a threat of inflation by a substantial release of hoarded purchasing power at the point of 'normal' employment, the Pool would itself sell stocks at an upper limit of prices fixed and made known beforehand.

Provided the Pool bought only standardized storable goods in constant demand normally, there would be no objection to holding very large buffer stocks, though sales to the Pool below cost would not be likely in great volume except in a genuine trade depression. Even so, the money churned out by the Pool in payment would speedily reduce stocks again and restart the machinery of production. What is more to be feared is inflation on exhaustion of the Pool stocks beyond the point of 'normal' employment. But this is a danger common to all pump priming schemes, and could be adequately met by manipulation of the bank rate or other orthodox measures.

Naturally, changes in the conditions of demand for and supply of particular selected goods, however standardized they were, might be expected to occur in the course of a single trade 'cycle'. Thus at the worst the Pool would be left with stocks of useful raw materials (for instance, structural steel at a time when the preference was for concrete houses) which would have to be sold at a monetary loss, or useful consumption goods (for instance, wooden furniture outmoded by cheaper metal) which could be given away to the needy. These losses have to be compared with the losses of unemployment. They could be reduced still further if the Pool bought and sold only in 'commodity units' or combinations of fixed quantities of various selected goods at, say £1,000 per unit. Variations in the market prices of particular items would then normally cancel out.

It remains to add that these proposals are not nearly as revolutionary as they sound. The dethronement of the bankers is long overdue, and is in fact nearly accomplished. The withers of the business community seem quite unwrung at the spectacle, and the bankers themselves have not put up much of a fight for it. The commodity currency scheme is perhaps the quickest automatic way of maintaining aggregate spending power. Though it involves a considerable problem of Government management, the operation of the scheme, once prices and commodities are set, is purely automatic, and requires little discretionary power. It is in this respect superior to many of the schemes at present in vogue.[1] The threat to the free economic system of disastrous booms and slumps is now overwhelming, and the record of remedial measures so far adopted is not reassuring. It may be guessed that only a very bold scheme, conceived in harmony with that system, can be expected to safeguard it from the probably wide economic fluctuations of the future.

FREE ACCESS TO THE MARKET

The first principle of restrictionism is to prevent free access to the market; one of the main objects of Government action in the free economy should be to preserve it. This obviously cannot mean that everybody should expect to buy or sell anything in any market however he likes. In the first place, not all goods are suitable for turning into private property for purchase or sale on the market. Underground minerals, for example, are a very doubtful case, particularly oil deposits or underground water, where exploitation of bore-holes or springs by one owner may prejudice the value of other owners' property. Further, not all wants are individual—few people want streets and parks quite to themselves, and most positively prefer others to use them too. Some goods are produced in conditions such as long hours and bad conditions of work, which are freely accepted by a few, but are intolerable and dangerous to the health of many. Government must lay down standards in these matters. Other goods are supplied under conditions which prevent the whole cost being collected from the user—roads, for example; or which burden someone who gets none of the benefit, as in the case of the Westminster brewery, which Queen Victoria disapproved of because it could be smelled from Buckingham Palace. Under such conditions the free market will not

[1] Cf. the wide discretionary powers required to operate the employment policy outlined in Cmd. 6527, 1944.

work effectively, and must be supplemented by compensation arrangements or supplanted altogether by Government action, the general principle being to stretch the pricing system as far as it will go before bringing in the Government experts and arbitrators.

Of more practical importance is the question of the kind of competition which should be permitted once the market has opened. To some extent minimum standards of commercial morality are maintained by custom, and there is not much difficulty in restraining the grosser forms of force, fraud, and deliberate misrepresentation by suitable laws which tend to make a business career on the basis of these weapons outstanding in profits, but uncertain in duration. The difficulty is to draw the line at conduct which, though not morally wrong by accepted standards, yet defeats the operation of the free market. Professional moralists have unfortunately very little to say about the rights or wrongs of price discrimination by electrical suppliers, tied contracts for shoe machinery, or the block booking of films. What is even more surprising, however, is how little the stately generalizations of economists take account of these practices, at least in this country. The object of legislation in this matter should be to draw up general rules regulating these practices,[1] leaving them to be applied by an appropriate and adequately staffed Government authority, whose main business would be to make a continuous study [2] of the development of business practices

[1] The arguments for specifying offences in the rules, and so restricting litigation, are in 'Construction and Enforcement of the Federal Anti-Trust Laws', Handler, Monograph 38 of the U.S. Temporary National Economic Committee, 1941, p. 96. Cf. Miller, 'Unfair Competition', Cambridge, Mass., 1941, p. 410, which argues for the use of discretion by the regulating authority.

[2] Business practices are constantly being adapted under the pressure of economic change. The rules applicable to them should be changed accordingly.

which appeared to exercise a restrictive effect in particular markets. At present there is no such authority, though proposals for creating one have been made by several official investigators since 1919.

On one point, the authority will be clear from the outset. Trade practices which prima facie threaten the free market can in most cases be resolved into more or less open attempts to drive out or buy up competitors and set up a monopoly, which is the first natural impulse of an enterprising business man in a free economic system. It is tempting to conclude, and many economic writers have allowed the conclusion to be drawn, that the way to resist this is to try to produce 'perfect' competition all round. But this peculiar state is, of course, in practice about as attainable as perfect truth, and perhaps equally undesirable even if it could be attained. In face of expert salesmanship, the facts of geography, and the natural laziness of the consumer with an unreasonable affection for the corner shop, various degrees of imperfect competition will inevitably obtain—that is to say, people in one part of the market will go on buying things at high prices which they know they might get cheaper somewhere else. Contrary to accepted opinion, perfect competition is not characteristic of, and certainly not essential to, the free economic system, under which people may be as slow or as negative in their response to the stimulus of price movements as they can afford. No doubt in special cases, where the experience of instantaneous adjustments is extensive and the apparatus for dealing with them is well developed, as in the international grain markets or the markets for securities and foreign exchange, dealings may become almost perfectly competitive; but apart from those who like to change their milk supplier twice a day and get paid by the minute, nobody in his sense would want perfect competition generalized, and no Government body could enforce it even if it were wanted. The richer society becomes, the more willing people will be to disregard the loss of 'efficiency' which comes from the lack of instantaneous adjustment to economic change.

The characteristics of 'workable' competition,[1] which can be enforced, as distinguished from perfect competition, which cannot, are free entry for all comers, a state of potential competition in all markets, however safe they may appear to those supplying them, a state of real competition from substitute goods which technical development is constantly throwing up in what Schumpeter calls 'the perennial gale of creative destruction',[2] and plurality of producers. No producer must feel strong enough to be able to fix the price within wide limits regardless of the action of other producers, and anyone who thinks he can add to the supply at or under the prevailing price should be permitted to do so. The general rule is that competition should be lively enough to keep the producer on his toes, but not fierce enough to discourage investment.

The only important departure from these broad principles arises out of the generalized form of the 'infant industry' argument, according to which industries which cannot get a start because of the size, riskiness, and long-term nature of the investments they require, should be given some form of statutory protection—from foreign competition by a tariff on imports, from home competition by some variant of the patent system. But experience shows that such exceptions should be scrutinized with extreme care. Patents are only too often turned into permanent blocking devices which impede economic progress instead of accelerating it. And in a rich industrial country the plethora of capital seeking investment in times of peace casts a certain doubt

[1] Cf. 'Concept of Workable Competition', J. M. Clark, *American Economic Review*, June 1940.

[2] Cf. his 'Capitalism, Socialism, and Democracy', London, 1942.

on claims that no one can be found to finance an undertaking which in time offers a reasonable prospect of commercial success. If there is not a reasonable prospect of success it is not obvious why the community should be expected to share the risk by consenting to restrictions in the present for problematical benefits in the future.

'Workable' competition is thus, as the name implies, a modest and essentially practical aim. The absence of price warfare is not necessarily a sign of a failure to reach it; nor is high-pressure salesmanship and optimistic advertising, so long as the consumer can test the claims for himself; nor is idle productive capacity, even though prices may be high enough to cover the cost of maintaining it in slack periods, and therefore higher than the strict competitive level in busy periods. Nobody in his senses would want to break down the structure of building firms, for example, because they cannot use in winter all the capacity they need in summer.

On the other hand, not all forms of imperfect competition are compatible with workable competition. In the case of statutory monopolies, particularly where the undertaking is not completely State-owned, there is the strongest presumption of exploitation of the public, since potential competition is carefully ruled out and competition from substitutes is usually weak. Voluntary agreements between a majority of the firms in a whole industry to fix prices and exclude outsiders are prima facie an infraction of the rules of workable competition; so is the domination of a whole industry by one giant firm. Anti-monopoly legislation is required to outlaw the first and break up the second.

Protests against the dispersal of concentrations of economic power, which is required by anti-monopoly legislation, are nowadays based less on the classical analogies with the unscrambling of eggs and more on the wanton sacrifice of economies from large-scale production. The spokesmen for monopolistic firms explain that it is the existence of these economies in particular industries which either forces the industry into the monopolistic mould because it is only when production is carried on in a single firm that the output is produced at lowest cost, or else concentrates production in a very few giant firms which, if they compete at all with one another, tend to engage periodically in destructive price warfare where staying power is no measure of productive efficiency and only the general public is the final loser in the long run.

Certain doubts about the first argument arise from the fact that investigations made in the country of giant businesses, the United States, do not show that giant corporations are more efficient (i.e., have lower unit costs) than medium or small businesses.[1] In fact, they seem more often to be less efficient. They may be more *profitable*—though this is not invariable either—but it is not to be assumed that their profits are necessarily a consequence of efficiency; they may be the result of monopolistic exploitation. The decisive reason for the very large amalgamations in the U.S. industrial world has been the profits from refinancing operations rather than increasing efficiency. And a good deal has to be set down to the mere lust for power on the part of those at the top.

Doubts about the second argument spring from the fact that in practice industries often do come to be dominated by a few giant firms, which, as in the U.S. automobile industry, neither amalgamate nor engage in price wars, but compete strongly in the consumer market nevertheless, and have to admit an occasional new-comer to their ranks from time to time. So long as the firms remain separate and entry to the industry is free, there is always the influence of

[1] 'Relative Efficiency of Large, Medium-Sized, and Small Business', Monograph 13, U.S. Temporary National Economic Committee, 1941.

potential competition in the background to prevent serious exploitation; and this influence can be strengthened at will if the law imposes an arbitrary limit on the size of firms. It is doubtful whether the high limit which in practice would be sufficient to guarantee workable competition would involve any considerable reduction in efficiency; and even if it did, some reduction is quite acceptable as a necessary cost of maintaining the free system.

AN END OF RESTRICTIONISM

It is not to be supposed that with the promulgation of a new system of rules, the economic game—still less the players—will be purged of all wickedness at once. But in an economic system in which we all get a reasonably fair start, in which no one need want for the necessaries of life, and millionaires have a vital interest in preventing each other from exploiting the rest of us, it ought to be possible, and certainly would be desirable, to begin a vigorous pruning campaign against the tangled thicket of restrictionist practices in which the present productive machinery has to function.

For example, most of the present restrictions on access to occupations, apart from those connected with the minimum necessary training period, could and should be abolished. In a society which was only moderately sensible there would seem to be a certain appeal to common sense in the general rule that those who think they can do a job should not be prevented from trying if they can find an employer willing to give them a trial. Certainly nobody should be refused access to a job in the interest of a particular industrial or professional group.

There is equally no good reason why consumers should not get what they want within the widest limits—provided they are made to pay whatever it costs to produce. If they change their minds frequently, as they are apt to do in rich and progressive countries, production should be organized to follow them—for an appropriate fee. The fee should be negligible for changes between firms, larger for changes between industries, and largest for changes requiring new investments—either by savers in particular sorts of capital or by workers in particular sorts of skill. A useful ingredient of the fee might well be the cost of hiring workers for a minimum statutory period of, say, six months.

Participants in the productive process should be left free to dispose of their reward with the fewest restrictions. Thus the individual choice between spending and saving should be quite free, the Government taking off-setting measures as required in the general interest if collective savings were excessive or inadequate. There should be no law against putting money under the bed or into bank deposit accounts, fixed assets and titles thereto, retail businesses or old socks. But there should be a complete ban on investment in industries of the public utility type, where there are very large economies of scale and such heavy initial investments that 'workable' competition is impossible to maintain. In such cases outright Government ownership is the only solution of the problem of concentrated and irresponsible economic power. But the number of such industries is much smaller than is usually supposed.

No doubt it sounds nowadays very startling to suggest that there should be wide freedom to start in business in whatever locality seems most favourable to the enterpriser, who will divert land to his particular purpose by bidding up the price of it to a level determined by the urgency of the demand for his products. There is the distinct risk, however, that *Government* moves to locate business, perhaps in special areas of concentrated poverty or concentrated unemployment, will become the subject of political pressure, however well-intentioned; and the safer procedure is to free the channels *out* of the special area or the special industry, rather than to make it more tolerable for people to stay there. It is nevertheless clear that the market for industrial sites functions very ineffectively at present, not so much because of peculiarities in land itself, but because the enterpriser seldom pays all of the cost of production in a given locality, and in particular he does not pay the 'social costs' attributable to production. There is a large and varied range of such costs. At one extreme is the cost of unemployment insurance, which is not adjusted appropriately to industries of varying employment records and does not discourage as it should the undue concentration in one place of a specialized industry liable to heavy unemployment at particular times. At the other extreme there is the cost of removing industrial refuse, cleansing polluted rivers, and removing other alleged public nuisances, such as the smell of the Westminster brewery. In many cases these costs are borne by the public authorities—if the job gets done at all; and in cases where it does not get done, the 'costs' of putting up with the consequences are generally borne by the poor, whose standards of housing accommodation are for this reason, amongst others, deplorably low. The peculiarity of these odd arrangements is especially obvious when a firm moves out of a district at short notice and throws the cost of local public services, such as schools and hospitals, on to the local community, whose ability to pay for them will be much reduced. The commonsense solution is to make each firm bear its proper share of such costs by means of direct local taxation levied for beneficial local expenditure.

Apart from industrial location, the present arrangements for distributing living space do undoubtedly provide the town planners with a good prima facie case for stopping people from doing what they want to do where they want to do it. But the ground for their sort of restrictionism is not, as they imagine, that the builders of slums are more wicked than the rest of us, but that there is, and always has been, such a scandalous disparity between the housing that the rich can easily pay for and that the poor can afford. Again the remedy is not restrictions on building activity, but a change in the distribution of income.

There is every reason why savers, once having invested their capital, should be free to move it elsewhere if they want to. There is thus a good deal to be said for the proposal that much larger parts of the general reserves of limited companies should be paid back to shareholders, who could invest them elsewhere instead of putting them back automatically into the business. At the same time, nobody should be free to abuse the facilities of the capital market to concentrate economic power by the 'pyramiding' of holding companies, leaving the voting control in the hands of a few at the top. A ban on limited companies owning one another's shares would stop this practice, though there would obviously have to be an exemption for bona-fide investment trusts. And if the proportion of non-voting fixed interest bearing securities in the capitalization of limited companies was also rigidly fixed at a low figure, extreme concentration of capital could be made costly and uncertain and therefore unattractive.

The above illustrations are not intended to represent any systematic philosophizing about the new world, but to point the way to certain essential jobs of intellectual house-cleaning which must be done if the new world of the second half of the twentieth century is not to be a slightly sillier, and ultimately much sadder version of the old one of the first half. Above all, it should be clear that what is wanted is not a reversal of the genial humanitarian currents which set in a hundred years ago, when it first became obvious that nineteenth-century industrial capitalism had its seamy side; even less do we need to abandon faith in the long-cherished practice of Western civilization of letting people find the road to their own particular economic Heaven in their own particular way. What is needed in the warm-hearted planners of new worlds is simply the admission that arrangements for stopping work, reducing production, blocking trade, and restricting enterprise are not obviously the best way to make everybody better off, and are a particular disservice to the needy; and that the end of social justice is rather more likely to be served by re-distributing the product when the economic machine has had the chance to produce its maximum under the freest conditions than by tinkering with various parts of the works in isolation and thereby putting the brake on the whole. The future intellectual activities of reformers should undergo a change of emphasis. Their proper sphere is how to make production more, not less; their goal is not the perfect marketing scheme, the guileless cartel, or the harmless import quota, but the free market, the informed consumer, the venturesome enterpriser, and—last but decidedly not least—the perfect income tax.

CHAPTER 9

PRESENT PROSPECTS

THOSE who have difficulty in understanding the many quaint and bizarre features of the pre-war economic system when confronted with what common sense suggests the system ought to be, will be reassured to some extent when they recollect that more than half of the period 1919–39 was occupied in recovering from the first World War and preparing for the second. The cynics who claim that man is a munition-making animal cannot easily be answered from the facts of the inter-war period. The present generation may perhaps get some sympathy from its happier successors for having to devote so much constructive thought to the creation of an economic system suitable to the 'normal' times in which they (and, alas, so many previous generations) lived, when on the average people were either getting over one war or getting ready for the next.

However fair the distant harmonies suggested in the previous chapter, no one with any knowledge of the actual course of events after 1918 can regard the present prospects of sensible economic policy after the war as anything but dark and drear. In effect, the nature of the problems of economic demobilization and resettlement will be such as to rule out any real choice for some years after the war, and the methods which will have to be adopted for dealing with them will inevitably prejudice the choice when it is made.

ECONOMIC DEMOBILIZATION

Enough has been said in Chapter 1 to indicate that economic demobilization after a major war is not merely a matter of releasing all economic controls a few months after the Armistice. By an unfortunate and even dangerous coincidence, recovering from a total war, like preparing for one, is unquestionably a collectivist task in which various drastic and far-reaching Government interventions are essential. This does not necessarily mean reproducing the conditions of the Controller's Paradise, in which everything is forbidden which is not compulsory. But it does involve adequate recognition of the fact that, under modern conditions of war and near-war, tremendous economic changes must be brought about with a speed and comprehensiveness which the peace-time scale of remuneration to business men and workers could not possibly secure; and that the payment of larger sums to those in a favoured position, even if they were adequate, would not be tolerated. In the same way, the conditions of economic demobilization imply such drastic and unpredictable changes spread over a short period that Government intervention is essential to bring them about in a way which minimizes the fortuitous gains and losses which would otherwise result. The chief difference of the present demobilization period from the last one is that the changes are likely to be more drastic and less predictable.

In 1939 the war-makers could hardly fail to profit from the lessons of experience. In this, as in most of the other belligerent countries, the degree of economic mobilization since then has been far greater than in 1914–18, and far greater economic powers passed to the Government at a very early stage to transfer labour and resources quickly into war production. It seems probable, therefore, that, regardless of the promises of politicians and the wishes of their constituents, the 'unwinding' of the war economy will be a longer and more complicated process than it was last time. There will be the same problems, different only in degree from those of 1918, of over-built industries, particularly of the iron and steel, engineering and shipbuilding group; though expansion in particular sections—as for instance in aluminium fabrication—may have been greater this time, and the re-location of industrial capacity away from strategically vulnerable sites may very well complicate the task of plant disposal after military needs are past. In addition, there will be new problems resulting from new powers of control for which there is no precedent, such as those under the Concentration of Industry scheme and the Essential Work Orders. And, certainly not least important, there will be the problem of what to do with the controllers themselves—that is, the larger and much more powerful bureaucracy built up this time on the scale appropriate to total war.

Any substantial relief from the pressure of these problems will be obtained only under conditions which, however inevitable they may be regarded by diplomatists and other professional sceptics, will be viewed by the man in the street with something like despair. If demobilization is *not* complete, and the decision is taken as part of the Peace Settlement to maintain large armed forces afterwards, industrial conversion may perhaps be less troublesome than in 1918. But an exceedingly large military establishment will be required to bring much economic relief. The enormous rates of wastage of war equipment in war-time compared with peace-time make it likely that quite substantial forces could be maintained from a very small part of present armament manufacturing capacity. And the rather slight inducement to doing business in a peace-time world in which the principal nations face each other armed to the teeth can be gauged to a nicety because there was so much experience of it before 1939.

On the side of demand, the very effectiveness of the controls produced a much tighter restriction of the market for civilian goods much earlier, and shortages have been increased by the results of air attack. Arrears of civilian consumption of housing, furniture, clothing, and other goods in common demand are now much greater than they were in the corresponding period last time. 'Austerity' is a very modern military virtue; and, unfortunately, the more successfully it is practised during the war, the greater the problem bequeathed to the reconstruction period afterwards. The superior effectiveness of financial controls this time and the more widespread War Savings campaign have caused very large reserves of purchasing power to accumulate in the hands of the consuming public for use in the post-war years. Given the war-time system of high money rewards for high output, freedom from inflation in war-time has in practice only meant postponing the real problems of inflation till after the war.

The economic keynote of the immediate post-war period is therefore, on this showing, likely to be chronic shortages of consumer goods coupled with large accumulations of money to buy them with. The danger of the runaway monetary factor turning the whole conversion period into an inflationary boom even wilder than that of 1919–20 is obvious.

An internal boom in this country at present would be objectionable for reasons quite special to the time, and originating in the peculiarities of the British external economic position. Owing to the loss of some of the principal sources of pre-war revenue from abroad, notably ships and foreign investments, and the addition of large new liabilities, it will be desirable, if the country is to balance its accounts, for the value of imports to be as small as possible and the value of exports to be as large as possible. It remains to add that an internal boom would raise money prices, draw in imports, and cut down exports, which is the very opposite of what is required.

It is safe to assume that the critical point of all these difficulties, by a perverse coincidence not uncommon in economic matters, will come in the early part of the post-war transition period. Shortages would then be at their worst, particularly in the case of some imported raw materials like timber, rubber, and oil. The effect of war-time increases in productivity due to new technical methods, which in the long run might be expected to tell heavily in peace-time production, would then be at its minimum. Unfortunately, budgetary difficulties are also likely to be most serious at this time, as the Government will be under pressure from business men for the reduction of taxation on the one hand, and faced with demands for the continuation of war-time subsidies (especially on food), the payment of War Damage claims, income-tax credits, and Service gratuities on the other.

Unbalanced budgets followed on the last war; and an inflationary boom developed in 1920. But the policies of 1920 are now completely out of court. The belief that the official deflationist programme after 1920 was responsible for the post-war depression and the slow recovery thereafter is now so firmly rooted, and has been so greatly strengthened by subsequent monetary experience after 1931, that any serious attempt to deal with the next post-war inflation by the methods of 1920 is unlikely, to say the least. The most probable outcome is a continuation of the economic controls of war-time well on into the period of peace, until the point is reached when production begins to overtake arrears and the period of acute scarcities, not only in Great Britain but throughout the trading world, comes to an end. On the most favourable assumptions, it is difficult to believe that this point can be reached in less than 3–4 years from now.

RESTRICTIONISM IN THE POST-WAR YEARS

It would be the extreme of optimism to suppose that while something like a war economy is being operated in the early years of the peace, the problems of restrictionism will admit of any drastic treatment. The close co-operation of the organized economic groups—enormously strengthened during the war—with the official controlling agencies will be more than ever necessary once the general feeling of national emergency has worn off. The terms which the groups may offer to the Government for such co-operation may indeed be higher than in war-time; but in any case it would invite administrative paralysis to antagonize them. The awkward fact has to be faced, therefore, that we are in for a period of quite inevitable Government interventions on almost a war-time scale, with little prospect that the attendant embarrassments familiar from the experience of the inter-war period will be at all reduced.

Indeed, a further embarrassment is likely to be added. The controlled economy, while essential for getting over a modern war, is also apt for preparing for one. The claim that the free system is about the best economic guarantee of peace in a world of nation states that can well be devised, and that real peace is essential to its proper functioning, has been well and often argued in the nineteenth century. But the defects of the free system when peace is threatened have been made, in modern times, glaringly obvious. *Si vis bellum para pacem*, to put the ancient strategical tag in a modern dress, is a poor maxim except for long wars of endurance during which the contestants live on their fat. Those who adopted it before 1939 ran enormous risks, and some lost all.

Thus, if the Peace Settlement is a bad one, the claims of the restrictionists will be based on unassailable strategical grounds. Indeed, if a general view develops that the next few years are but one more breathing-space between two major world wars, the maintenance of freedom of any kind, economic or other, will be not only beyond hope, but probably beyond reason too. Restrictionists who base their case on the need for military preparedness will find no answer to that case in this book. Here it is assumed, perhaps not entirely without warrant at the time of writing (December 1945), that the Settlement will seem to most people reasonably durable and to promise a long period of reasonable international stability. In these circumstances the maintenance of all the formidable and complicated apparatus of Government economic controls (no doubt for the most unexceptionable economic reasons) by one great nation at the beginning of a period which is to usher in the Great Peace of the twentieth century may well be thought a little suspicious by some of the others, if not a standing threat to international security. It may, of course, be a pure coincidence that import restrictions and monetary regulations which are demonstrably necessary to maintain equilibrium in the Balance of Payments also have the effect of protecting strategically necessary industries. For this reason, it would have been difficult, for instance, to have objected to the German Government making wool out of milk, silk out of wood, and cotton out of coal and chalk, and taking the necessary restrictionist measures to this end. What possible harm could have come, as the Germans might have argued in 1939, from the German Government taking a census of artificial teeth and ordering the gold ones to be surrendered forthwith to the Reichsbank in order to help re-establish the Balance of Payments? Or sending German Boy Scouts around to pick up beech-nuts? No doubt very good economic reasons *could* have been given by Great Britain to the West Indies for her subsidies to sugar beet, by Germany to the Dutch East Indies for her subsidies to buna, and by Australia to the United States for her import duties on motor-cars. But it would always be very difficult to tell whether the real reason for making everything out of local sawdust and mud was economic adaptation during the reconstruction period or strategical insurance.

CONCLUSION

The fact that economic reconstruction after the war will have to be undertaken in conditions calling for Government intervention on an embarrassingly large scale merely enhances the essential wisdom and the ultimate attraction of a logically consistent régime of economic freedom. But it complicates the task of attaining it. Nobody supposes that the present and prospective beneficiaries of restrictionism are going to resign their claims in a sudden access of sweet reasonableness immediately the war is over, however slender the ground may be on which they are put forward. Equally, it would be unwise to underrate the misgivings of the real victim—namely, the general public—on this subject. Plainly some way must be found which, while accepting the case for economic controls during the immediate post-war years, puts an ultimate end to restrictionism in the name of the general welfare without causing a mass revolt of the groups whose interests are adversely affected.

The orthodox method would be to buy off opposition by compensating the interests on the basis of their established income expectations, finance being provided by Government borrowing or by income-pooling, as ingeniously suggested by Hutt. But it cannot be said that all the expectations concerned were particularly well established before the war, and a good many have been grievously disappointed since. It appears that a gradual relaxation of restrictions and withdrawal of special privileges over a long period would give the same results and would be more manageable politically. The most straightforward case would be that of a group which relies on the protection of an *ad valorem* import duty. The competitive price of the product (on the world market) would be known, the money benefits of the restriction to the home industry could therefore be calculated exactly, and the reduction of protection could be brought about by gradual and proportionate stages over several years. This suggests a workable principle for the relaxation of other Government restrictions in favour of particular groups. A money value should be placed on the income derived from them by the beneficiaries, and they should be gradually relaxed in stages measured by movements in the price of the product, for example, or by the numbers of new sellers admitted to the market in relation to the number desiring admission.

At the same time, the Government should give notice of its intention to press forward with a legislative programme (which, whatever the intentions, could certainly not be completed for several years) regulating competition, breaking up or buying out monopolies, and setting up a Government agency for administering the law against restraint of trade and investigating business practices which appeared to infringe them. And a Ministry of real Information should be set up, dedicated, not, as at present, to the exploitation of the black arts of salesmanship itself, but to restraining others from doing so to the public hurt, as well as providing the fullest possible statistical and other factual information about employment and industrial prospects over as wide an area as might be desired. A scheme for the proper regulation of the money supply should be got into working order before the onset of the first post-war depression, and the campaign against inequalities should be begun with an early attack on the problem from both ends.

The sort of economic system implied in these proposals involves no very violent and immediate disturbance of established expectations or of existing institutions. It does not rely on any particular Government to set it going, but on a new public attitude to restrictionism; and it obviously cannot be maintained by any particular set of rules regardless of place and time, but only by constant vigilance and by constant adaptation of the rules to the facts of economic development in the light of the basic principles of the free system.

The emphasis on a 'system' may appear undue. If men were angels, no doubt the most ramshackle economic arrangements, perhaps even those of the pre-war years, could be made to work successfully. Indeed, it is possible that for several years after the war, persons of angelic temper may be found in Government Departments and in various trade bodies dispensing even-handed justice to the citizen. But in an unregenerate post-war world it may be doubted whether virtue so tried could survive for long; and the consequences of a permanent Lucifer at the Board of Trade or in the Iron and Steel Federation are awful to contemplate. It is not preoccupation with the superior logic of a particular system but mere common prudence which suggests that it is best to avoid putting fallible men into official positions where they can do immense harm or immense good to particular economic interests.

At a time when the strategical points of power in business and administration are more valuable and more attractive than ever before, the need for watchful democratic government is crucial. But its quality is deteriorating. The present demonstration of the effectiveness of collective action in war—Governments excel in making war—has deepened men's already excessive faith in political action and created the illusion that there are no limits to the power of the State to change the conditions of life. There may perhaps be no great harm in passing laws ordering that all men must be reasonable, but there are some fields in which it is not only useless but dangerous to get the Government to 'do something about it'.

'In 1874', wrote Graham Wallas, 'British Liberalism, after forty-four years of almost uninterrupted power, lost its control over British policy and lost it largely because its conception of liberty was inadequate for the solution of any really difficult political problem.' This is the statement of a world-wide tendency, far transcending the fate of any political party, a reminder that the liberal-thinking world has been on the defensive for too long. The claim that the free economic system in its nineteenth-century form will not work does not dispose of the case. The political value of free democracies at the present stage of the world's history is so great that their continuous degeneration through economic interventionism may be of the most vital importance. Well-wishers of the Common Man must think again. Compromise may mean monopoly capitalism all round—for a time. But the present choice is clearly provisional, and seems merely to have substituted for what has been called the organized rapacity of the nineteenth century the much more insidious and ultimately more deadly principle of organized ca' canny in the twentieth. In the long run jumping out of the frying-pan into the fire will not avail.

On all these matters there is much to be said for more public enlightenment. Unless they are put on inquiry beforehand, ordinary people are not apt to be very curious about the particular social and economic system in which they live. Though they are prepared to make any sacrifice to defend it when the time comes, most of them can be persuaded only with difficulty to take some small step in times of quiet to avoid the necessity for sacrifices later. The time for the small steps will soon come.

For Product Safety Concerns and Information please contact our EU representative GPSR@taylorandfrancis.com Taylor & Francis Verlag GmbH, Kaufingerstraße 24, 80331 München, Germany